MW01067600

"*Extraordinary Healing is th*
transformational healing, ent
place. Moreover, because of
with yoga and healing, the n.
wisdom not ordinarily found in a clinical or self-help book. Here
you learn how to use energy therapies, such as EFT, along with
powerful hypnotic inductions and imagery tools. You learn
releasing and regression techniques as well as how to make and
use tapes. A very spiritual, practical and useful book by a skilled
clinician. Highly recommended."

> – Philip Friedman, Ph.D.,
> Psychologist and Coach,
> Author of *Creating Well-Being*,
> Director of Foundation for
> Energy and Spiritual Healing

"*Thank you from the bottom of my heart. This beautiful work is*
transforming my life on a daily basis. I'd been going through the
most difficult time in my life. Now I find that I'm filled with
excitement and joy. I've learned more from this work in a short
while than I did in eight years of study at various universities and
institutions of higher learning."

> – Stacy Dryer, MA, Ph.D., Cht.

"*This work has helped me to transform my life and my*
consciousness. I recommend it to anyone seeking truth and love."

> – Maria Rivero, MD

Extraordinary Healing

TRANSFORMING YOUR CONSCIOUSNESS, YOUR ENERGY SYSTEM, AND YOUR LIFE

Marilyn Gordon

A Guidebook for Healing Yourself and Others with
Transformational Hypnotherapy and EFT
(Emotional Freedom Techniques)

WiseWord Publishing
Oakland CA

WiseWord Publishing
PO Box 10795
Oakland CA 94610

Printed in the United States of America
Book Design by Carla Radosta

ISBN 9781438241470

Dedication

*This book is dedicated
with love to you
on your path of awakening.
It is my wish that this book
will in some way make
a contribution to your journey.*

"This is the divine art of consciousness transformation.
First it explores and releases the difficulties.
Then it takes you to the next step in
your process of coming to light.
It calls upon the consciousness that is already
within you, and it invites you to experience,
release and transform whatever is in the
way of your enlightened self.
Underneath the 'play of light and shadows' is
pure consciousness, itself.
Underneath the anger, fear, grief, self-doubt, failure,
rightness and wrongness, there is a radiant core.
This is what we've come here to uncover.
Fortunately, we have all the necessary tools.
Healing is the work of a lifetime,
both a commitment and
an ultimate joy."

– Marilyn Gordon

Acknowledgements

I am deeply grateful to those who've supported this work and this book. My love, appreciation and thanks:

To Dianne Kathryn Short for her friendship, loving kindness, enduring support and editorial assistance.

To Ronda Rice, Liz Kaminski and Kim Markison for their creativity, love, and support.

To Ormond McGill for his friendship and inspiration.

To Priscilla Stuckey for her editorial expertise.

To Carla Radosta for her great creativity and assistance in formatting this book.

To Mark Douglas for his generosity and for introducing me to the tapping techniques.

To Gary Craig for his lively innovations in the energy therapies.

To Dwight Damon for his professional support.

To Betty Moore-Hafter for her kindness and encouragement.

To Bart and Judy McLean for their shamanistic power.

To Brian Choate for his technical wizardry.

To Max Ashcraft for her friendship.

To the Worldwide Online Hypnotherapy Network for wisdom and community.

To my family members, who now reside on the Other Side: my mother for her encouragement, my father for his self-discipline and his legacy, my brother for his sweetness, my grandmother for her unconditional love.

To Nada Gordon for her creativity.

To my Aunt Phyllis and family for their love.

To Dr. Stephen Milligan and Dr. Harold Kristal for their care.

To the teachers at our school, for their great contributions.

To the thousands of clients and many students who've contributed their life experiences to the evolution of this work.

To Mata Amritananda Mayi, Ammachi, for her divine love and profound inspiration.

To all my teachers throughout the years.

I deeply thank you.

With love,

Marilyn Gordon

Contents

Part Two

From Darkness into Light:
Transformational Healing

Part Three

Higher Consciousness:
The Next Dimensions of Healing

Part Four

The Energy System

Part Five

Healing Processes for You to Do

Part Six

Techniques for Transformational Healing

Energy Therapy Variations — 233

Foreword
by Ormond McGill

This is a remarkable book. Years of professional practice have gone into its preparation. Marilyn Gordon's work is innovative, combining the spiritual and practical worlds. She writes in a very personal manner; it comes directly from expertise in working with thousands of clients and teaching many classes and workshops. She presents a combination of healing approaches for changing times, which together create "extraordinary healing."

This book addresses all levels of consciousness. It combines the vast subconscious resources of the deep inner mind with a way of working on the energy meridians. You'll notice that there are two main parts of this book. The first part contains timeless wisdom and healing stories. The second part invites you to learn in detail exactly how to do this work for both yourself and others.

In this book, you'll find answers to these questions and more: how we can be more aware as human beings, how we can handle the moment-to-moment obstacles from our minds and the stresses in our lives that incessantly appear, and how we can realize our spiritual identities.

These are the great questions of all time. I invite you to read on and experience the wisdom and joy of *Extraordinary Healing*.

Ormond McGill, PhD.
"Dean of American Hypnotists"
Palo Alto, CA
2000

Foreword
by Gary Craig

I was privileged to meet Marilyn Gordon in 1998 at my advanced energy healing seminar in San Francisco where she proceeded to demonstrate the powerful blending of hypnotherapy and the new energy techniques. It was a marvel to watch and, fortunately, we caught it on videotape.

My eyes have been wide open ever since.

She has gone on to innovate still further and thus take her procedures to new levels. This book displays those innovations in a delightful, easy to read manner and reflects the skill, caring and competency that is uniquely Marilyn.

One of my favorite sayings is that we are on the ground floor of a new Healing High Rise. When we finally get to the Penthouse, I suspect Marilyn will be waiting there for us.

Gary Craig
Founder, Emotional
Freedom Techniques (EFT)
The Sea Ranch, CA
2000

Part One

Extraordinary Healing:

Combining the Subconscious,
Higher Consciousness,
the Mind and
the Energy System

There is a revolution happening in healing.

The human condition can be a profound challenge. Even William Blake, as he wandered from street to street in his own era, saw everywhere "marks of weakness, marks of woe." We are all looking for solutions. We seek ways to handle our overwhelming emotions; we long for deeper spiritual strength and connection; we look for ways to overcome the numerous fears, obstacles and challenges of our lives.

Extraordinary Healing is dedicated to that purpose. It is, in fact, two books in one. It combines inspirational wisdom with a practical handbook of how to incorporate emotional, physical, mental and spiritual healing techniques into your daily life. Here is information on profound inner healing combined with a relatively new genre called "energy therapy," which works by tapping with the fingers on the energy meridians. The combination is miraculous. Many people have found their fears, grief, anger, physical pain, old habits and cravings, as well as other life obstacles either reduce considerably or completely disappear. Relationship issues, old wounds and traumas, lack of self-worth, anxieties, performance problems and many other challenges can be reduced or alleviated with these approaches. The technique is amazingly simple, and the results are often rapid.

This healing system embraces all levels of consciousness.

With the combined powers of your subconscious mind, higher consciousness, conscious mind and energy system, you can resolve the dilemmas of your life with skill and grace. You can do self-healing or work with someone else.

The *subconscious mind* is a repository of all that you have been and done. It's the storage place, the database, of all that has taken place in your experience. You can visit it and take a journey into its vast terrain. You can put it on "search mode"—ask it what you need to know at any given point in time. It's brilliant, and it'll take you exactly where you need to go. It's an inner card catalog, the Akashic records, the database of all time. It knows what you need to know, and if properly asked, it will retrieve and send you the information that will let you know the root causes of present experiences—and more.

Higher consciousness is a built-in enlightenment system. Through it, you experience the profundity of the universe. You come to know the brilliant light of all creation, ecstatic love, the great ability to stand back and view life from expanded states of awareness, extraordinary compassion—and all of it constitutes the healing power.

The *energy system* can be accessed with the appropriate keys. It's a system of meridians or energy pathways in your body. Getting in touch with this system can align your energy so that it runs smoothly, without any disruptions, within you. The ability to smooth out this electromagnetic energy will open you to healing your emotions, your thoughts, your physical body and your soul.

And because the quality of your thoughts naturally has a deep effect on your healing process, we also address your conscious mind.

The techniques for reaching all these systems are found in this book. You'll learn how to reach these parts of your being and what to do with the material you find.

The three stages move from darkness into light.

You can experience the three stages of inner transformation as you heal anything in your life that is clouding the experience of your true self. The stages are: *Experience – Release – Transform.*

You'll see how to first "experience your own experience" fully. Then you'll find extraordinary ways of releasing your experience. You'll then be able to uncover the shining jewels that are lying inside. These are love, joy, peace, light, compassion and enlightenment.

The following story illustrates these stages. A woman in her late seventies named Anna was angry with her mother for not giving her love. She had once overheard her mother telling someone that she never really wanted to have a child. Anna had been in therapy for seven years; yet something was still in her way, as she continued to stew in her anger.

We first addressed her energy system with a process of tapping with the fingertips on specific points on the body while simultaneously speaking about the situation, and this decreased the intensity of her anger. The topic she spoke about as she tapped on these points was "feeling controlled by my mother." After several rounds of tapping, the feeling left her completely. The release was astounding. She was able to go even further. She glided into a state of deep relaxation, and she saw herself swimming in an exquisite underwater scenario. Here she could move with total freedom. She was washing away the rage and was now flowing with gorgeous colors, animals and plants of the ocean.

The tapping process had made this inner experience accessible to her. She was able to enter a transcendent state after she'd released the baggage of emotions she'd been carrying all her life. She was able, through more tapping during her relaxation process, to see her experience with her mother through completely new eyes. She saw that both she and her mother were doing the best they could, given all the experiences of their lives, and that forgiveness was totally within her reach.

The epiphany came when she was able to share this experience with her mother, who was no longer alive on this earth. She told her mother that she finally saw things differently. She told her mother that she'd now released her from all she'd thought she was. Because she had prepared the way for this through all the previous work she'd done, she was ready for a shift, an opportunity for liberation. Love flowed freely and exquisitely between them. This was the connection she'd been wishing for all her life.

This is not an isolated story. Extraordinary healing occurs by addressing all levels of consciousness. Complete directions for doing all phases of this process are contained in parts 5, 6 and 7 of this book. You can do it with and for yourself, or you can do it with others. You may even find yourself entering into realms of the miraculous.

The way out is through.

This is a system for healing whatever in your life is obscuring the light of your soul. The results are both practical and transcendental. Its philosophy is that "the way out is through," that there is nothing inherently bad or wrong with anything you're undergoing. Everything is material worthy of being paid attention to. Everything you're experiencing is an opportunity for understanding and self-knowledge.

After experiencing whatever you need to experience, you are then able to release whatever you need to release. Paying attention to your experience may create a release in itself. You'll learn in this book additional ways to powerfully release from yourself obstructions that are covering your light and your peace.

Inside your own being is an essence that is ready to shine beyond the difficulties that life presents. In this book you'll receive tools and techniques and ways of extraordinary healing that will allow you to know the joy that you naturally carry as a seed within your consciousness.

Ancient roots combine with modern technologies.

One of the greatest ancient healers was a Greek priest-physician by the name of Aesclepius. He had two daughters with familiar names: Hygeia and Panacea. It's said that his father was Apollo, the god of healing. When Aesclepius died, healing temples were erected all through the Greek States and the Roman Empire. Very special events took place in these healing temples. Sick people would come, and they'd be bathed and cleansed before they would go into the temple; then they'd be dressed in white clothes, and they'd be shown into the inner chambers. They'd meet the priest-physicians, who instructed them to lie down with a statue of Aesclepius right by the bedside and go into a very deep sleep, in which they would dream a healing dream. In this dream they were told they might come into contact with Aesclepius himself who'd tell them the nature of their problems and the remedies. In the morning, most of the time, they'd know exactly what they needed for their healing. Many thousands of healings took place in this way.

This was an early form of what we now know as deep inner healing or transformational healing or hypnotherapy. It was a way of going deeply into the inner chambers of the soul and finding a great resource of inner wisdom and truth. Transformational healing is a way of turning darkness into light by working with higher consciousness to heal the difficulties of life.

We combine deep inner healing with ways of working with the energy system. Approximately 2300 years ago, *The Yellow Emperor's Classic of Internal Medicine* appeared in China. It described principles of working with the meridians or energy pathways that have since been developed in many different cultures. Parts 4 and 7 of this book explain one particular technique. This is a way of tapping with the fingers on specific energy points while using special healing language in order to bring a smooth flow of electrical charge to the human energy system. We have combined these techniques with deep inner healing.

A woman named Ruth lived in varying states of panic. She was breathless and on the verge of crying. Ruth was almost 60, and she hyperventilated and got panic attacks in enclosed spaces such as elevators and tunnels. She was at her wit's end, sometimes waking up with this terror and having great difficulty breathing. Sometimes she thought she would die.

We began to tap her for her fear of suffocating, fear of dying, and for not being able to breathe. As we tapped, she began to breathe freely, and her fear left her. With a process of deep relaxation, she was able to go more deeply to pay attention to whatever her deep inner mind wanted her to know about this problem she was having. As she relaxed, she went back to a time a number of years ago when she'd been in a store. Her son was waiting there for her, and he was eating a snack. She took a bite if it, and she began to choke. She couldn't breathe, and she thought she'd die. Her son found her husband who was close by, and he told his son, "We don't have time to call 911. She'll be gone before they get here." On the third attempt with the Heimlich Maneuver, he was successful, and the snack became dislodged and shot out of her mouth.

Ruth was saved, but she carried this traumatic experience within her. It was a freeze-framed picture inside of a terrorized woman who was dying by suffocation. She hadn't remembered this incident, but the brilliant database of her deep inner mind gave her the information she needed to find an origin of her obsessive terror of not being able to breathe. Like the ancient supplicants who came to visit Aesclepius in their sleep states, she had been able to contact the source within her that told her a root of her distress.

Ruth had another revelation. She recalled a time when she and her family were caught in an elevator that had stopped. Her husband had begun to bounce up and down there, telling her that if the elevator fell, there would be giant springs at the bottom that would cushion them. This was no comfort to Ruth. It was a terror that never left her.

Inside, she contacted Gabriel the archangel who put his wings around her, and she began to glow with a spirit of protection. In her mind's eye, she also asked Gabriel to accompany her back into that old choking scene in the dressing room. Her family was no longer screaming with fear, and she experienced peace. Ruth also learned to pay more attention to her breathing, to do the tapping for herself if she ever needed to, and to recall this state of safety that resides naturally within her.

We're born with tendencies of the mind that we've come here to heal.

The deep inner mind is a vast storage place, an amazing database. It's an information system that contains all that has gone before, patterns, tendencies, and future pathways. It is the library of the Akashic Records, the books of infinity, on which our lives are written.

Eastern cultures have handed down knowledge of tendencies of the mind, called *vasanas* or *samskaras*, impressions that are imprinted on the subtle body, and brought into our experiences when they are triggered by something current. We bring these tendencies of the mind in with us when we're born, and they appear during our lives as our grounds of being. Some have *vasanas* or *samskaras*, tendencies that contain such thought forms as, "I'm not worthy. I can't do anything right." Or "I need to destroy myself or somebody else." Or "I'm so alone; I can't connect with anyone." There are even times when it is the

opposite extreme: "I think I'm better than everyone else."
All of these tendencies are, of course, distortions of truth.

The objective of our lives is to heal these tendencies, to
go beyond them into more enlightened states, in which
we know that we are connected with the Source of
ourselves and that behind all thought forms, there is an
inner core of profound wisdom and radiance.

Within the deep inner mind or subconscious are all
parts of ourselves, fragments that need attention, frozen
pictures in the soul. Within these fragments are old fears
and angers, grief and guilt. One woman, Sara, saw one of
her fragments as a woman in a cell. There was straw on
the floor, and it was almost totally dark both in the cell
and inside of her. She saw herself as distraught, emaciated,
neglected—even though she was an active, reasonably
healthy, successful woman. Inside of her was a freeze
frame, perhaps from another lifetime, perhaps from old
wounds of this lifetime that hadn't healed.

As you go deeply within, through the layers of being,
you can come face to face with these fragments of self,
asking who it is that's experiencing the fear, anger,
loneliness or grief. In this exploration, you find less
evolved parts of self that for eons have been asking to be
shown the way to the light.

When Sara found the woman in the cell, she was
reunited with a long lost part of herself, and she began to
connect this fragment with more enlightened states. Light
began to stream into the cell from a tiny window. She
found food there in a plate on the straw floor. More light

began to stream in, and she began to nourish herself with food for both her body and her spirit.

She had recovered a fragment and had begun to see it evolve. She was able to feel more whole. She didn't feel that there was this terribly suffering part inside of herself any longer. Soon after, the iron doors opened, and she became free of that cell completely. She was able to come home to herself and to reawaken the spiritual energy within her.

The union of deep inner healing and energy therapy creates a powerful synergy.

We have found powerful results in our explorations combining all levels of consciousness in our healing. Together they create a beautiful synergistic healing system.

One man, James, was obsessed by a relationship. He was in love with a woman—and she wanted "to be friends." For two years they did everything together. It wasn't a physical relationship, and it was strange for him to stay in a relationship that wasn't going anywhere. Still, everything he thought about had to do with her. His life was going downhill physically and emotionally. To add to this, she didn't treat him well; she said mean things to him, and he knew that now was the time to handle this so he could get on with his life. He was miserable, and it was time to take a major step.

We began tapping on his energy meridians for various issues:

- Anger at himself for being in this situation
- Despair
- Sadness (about not being what others wanted him to be, trying to be someone he's not, and not living his life for himself)
- The physical feeling of heaviness in his chest, eyes and throat

He began to forgive himself for not having an agenda for his own life, for misplacing it by attending to others' agendas more than his own. He came to know that his task was to become whole within himself, to live his own life and become deeply connected with his own essence.

As he relaxed into deep inner healing, he saw himself flying. He looked down and at first felt his own sadness. He saw it reflected in all the unhappy faces he saw below. He continued to fly, and the sadness shifted as he saw a magnificent madrone tree. For some reason, he felt love from that tree. He felt expanded, and he was able to go beyond all the sadness into the essence of love that was within him and have compassion for everyone. He was able to love and witness the transformation of the child he'd been and even of his depressed self. We tapped while he was in relaxation for some residues of sadness and fear, and he relaxed completely.

He'd been looking for this breakthrough—out of his depression and obsession. He found it. In subsequent sessions, we worked on his self-worth, feelings that he didn't deserve to feel so happy (as he was beginning to experience a new kind of joy). We tapped for a residual fear of failure. In further deep inner healing, we opened some bound up feelings that had manifested in his body.

In his mind's eye, he saw a Tibetan man on a horse, a deep spiritual symbol to him. He heard a bell ring, and he knew that it was ringing to awaken his consciousness. His Wise Mind said to him, "Be patient. Just keep going forward. It's time now for you to begin a new life."

What astounded me about James was the shift in his demeanor. The first time I saw him, he was contracted. He had a deep furrow in his brow and anger and sadness in his eyes. He answered me with choppy, terse, staccato sentences. The second time I saw him, he was smiling. The furrow in his brow was gone, and there was a radiance about him. He had deepened his connection with his own divine consciousness.

There is a compass that points us back to ourselves and opens our higher centers.

Often we find that we are "away from ourselves." We feel depleted or abandoned or alone, and it seems sometimes as if we're traveling in some dark forest with no idea how to get back home. Fortunately there are tools and techniques that provide a compass, pointing us back to ourselves. We can then open our higher centers, experience the fourth dimension, raise our vibration, and go beyond the appearance of things. We find our transcendent selves once again. When we do, we're able to stand back and see from an expanded perspective. We become centered, and our higher energy centers remember the experiences of ecstatic love, divine wisdom, deep compassion, and radiant light.

An emotional alchemy happens as we transform our fear into love and faith, the fire of rage into light, our grief into compassion and connection. It is then that we come back to ourselves.

A man in his late fifties we'll call Sam, was at a point in his life in which he'd succeeded in doing what he wanted to do in the world. He raised his family and earned a good living as a computer programmer, but he wondered to himself, "What's the purpose of the whole shebang? There should be something with more meaning." He thought it might be that he should strive to change his career, but he really knew that what he needed to do was to see inside himself.

We tapped on his energy meridians, and he was able to overcome the feeling of not knowing in which direction to turn. Then he broke through the barrier of a nervous feeling of uncertainty, and then he overcame the concrete rock of a barrier that kept him in a state of disconnection.

As he began to go into deep relaxation, he saw leaves and a stream in his mind's eye. He made a connection with his inner wisdom. It said, "Just see what's around you. You have everything you need. You just need to let go and see what's there. Just let go and appreciate yourself as you are. Everything is as it should be. Just listen to the birds and watch the streams. You'll be given all the answers you need. Just be open to accept them."

In first moving through his barriers, releasing them, and making contact with his higher being, he was able to make a true breakthrough. He said that he felt as if a dam had broken. He knew that more wisdom and understanding would now come to him, as he remained in contact with his expanded self.

You're able to move gracefully from darkness into light by working with the gifts you have within yourself: your subconscious mind, higher consciousness, conscious mind and energy system. As you combine the new technologies for healing with ancient wisdom, you may truly find that this combination has a profound effect upon your life.

In parts 2 and 3, we'll talk about transformational healing, which is a way of moving from darkness into light. In part 4, we'll explore the energy system. In parts 5 through 7, you'll receive many techniques. But first, here's my story of how this work came to be.

My life has been transformed

Though it didn't always seem so at the time, everything I've done and been has been an essential part of the path I'm travelling on now. This path has been for me a fascinating, eventful one, filled with both very painful struggles and profound experiences of bliss and light. There were times when I knew that what I was doing was preparing me for something more expansive, and I called many of my old experiences "boot camp." I can now see that on this long and winding road, everything was geared to prepare me to do the work I'm doing now in the deep inner healing of the soul.

I've always had a penchant for the inner worlds. I must have been six or seven, when one day, at the suggestion of my artistic babysitter, I took black watercolor paint, spread it over a piece of paper and let it dry. When I held it up to the sun, I clearly remember seeing holy people wearing robes. I also loved the fairies who lived in thimbles and flowers. I loved the elves who sat on toadstools, and the little people. I loved a radio program called "Let's Pretend." I listened to it every Saturday morning. I loved my imaginary friends, Moo Boo and Savvy. They were wonderful. They lived under my bed, and they were my companions. I spent a lot of time inside myself playing these imagination games, and as I grew older, I kept the inner worlds alive.

When I was young, I had a recurrent vision of an Easter

egg with an opening through which I could walk inside. There I'd enter into a town of pastel houses that was from another realm. I could go there by closing my eyes and seeing myself climb into that egg and become transformed. I would walk along those pastel streets and feel uplifted. This was a purely magical world in which I became luminescent and filled with joy. Here I could move beyond my ordinary life.

Going into this egg was a way of entering an alternate reality that to this day holds great value for me. This world of the deepest imagination is the cousin of the world of higher consciousness. I now know that this alteration in consciousness contains the remedy for all of life's vicissitudes. When I later entered the world of healing, I saw that the love I had for my inner world as a child was not just a fairy tale. It was a way of moving into higher levels of knowledge—and healing the deepest difficulties of life.

When I was a young teen, something happened to my consciousness. I was sixteen, and it was if an incandescent light had suddenly been lit in my awareness. Maybe it was a flyer that I saw at a bus stop. I believe it was a Christian Science flyer—and it read, "Did you know that the mind can heal?." I took the flyer home, intrigued by the fascinating potential. At this time, even my choice of clothes changed—from multi-colors to black tops and tights and a single skirt that I wore almost every day. My mother was horrified. She hoped and prayed that this was just a stage. Actually, it was to be an outer symbol of the inner search I was on, my search for self-knowledge.

I had an English teacher at this time who was truly extraordinary, profoundly dedicated and serious about her teaching. She taught us Plato and Shakespeare, great short stories, and grammar. She'd been my teacher when I was about fourteen, but when I was sixteen, I was different, and I wrote a paper on *Candide*. She said, "Is this your paper? Did you write this yourself?" I told her that I had, and she was amazed. She recognized that something had truly transformed within me. Another one of my papers was an interpretation of a poem. It was a poem about a black boat that was floating on the waters of the ocean. It said, "The boat is death, floating on the ocean of time and all eternity." My early interest in symbolism like this impressed her. She said, "This is excellent. Subtract about twelve more adjectives, and this will be a creditable piece of work." She then put me in the after-school Shakespeare group. We sat and read *Hamlet* out loud. After that I read it six times, and not too long after that I went to college and studied English. I became an English teacher myself.

I too was dedicated. Like my English teacher I used to write paragraphs on the students' papers, commenting about their ideas and their writing, helping them with their thoughts or their own imaginations. I loved it. Sometimes I'd sit on top of the desk when I was teaching and hold deep conversations with the students. I introduced them to ways of looking at literature and their lives.

As time went on and I was teaching, some of the students began to riot in the schools. It was my fifth year of teaching. Some of the students would throw plates around the lunchroom. Students would fight in the hallways, and I would go and help break up fights. I mustered up all the adrenalin I could and went to help break up fights. Sometimes I would come home exhausted and in a kind of catatonic state. I'd sit in a chair and stare at the walls.

One day I was listening to some music after school. Jimi Hendrix was popular at that time, and one of his songs said, "With the power of soul, anything is possible." Those words inspired me with the deep sense that there was a soul power in me that could do anything. I also listened to Crosby, Stills and Nash, and one of their songs said, "Take the system and bow their heads." This ignited the spirit in me, impelling me to leave that life and return to California.

I lived in California in the '60s. I went to graduate school at the University of California for a while. The English Department's approach was too rigid for me. I wanted to explore William Blake's and Emily Dickinson's mystical metaphors, and some of the professors wanted me to pay attention to the diction and the meter. I left the graduate school, and soon after, I was married and had a baby girl. When things didn't work out, I took my daughter back to Chicago. I taught high school there until 1970. Then I decided to come back to California.

I stopped everything I was doing, and I began a whole new life. It was hard at first. I had to detoxify my body. My body was so stressed out from those last days in Chicago. I'd been on Fiorinal, an aspirin with a barbiturate. I smoked a pack of cigarettes a day and drank six cups of coffee. To start a whole new life, I had to release the old one from the very cells of my body. I was stressed from my own life, from my family life, from the situation in my environment and my work. I'd been going through a divorce. I'd had a difficult relationship. I had a small child. My brother was emotionally ill; my mother was sick. Everything that could go wrong went wrong in my life and in my family, and I was truly a basket case of stress. I yearned for relaxation. I had no idea how to relax. I used to go to the drug store and walk down the aspirin aisle to see if I could find new kinds to relieve my tension.

When I got to California in 1970, someone suggested, "Why don't you try yoga?" I didn't know too much about it. Someone said, "There's a class over on Dolores Street at the Integral Yoga Institute." I thought that maybe it could help me.

I went into the Integral Yoga Institute, and it was a landmark moment of my life. It was truly peaceful there. I loved the smell of fresh baked bread and clean wood and incense. We walked upstairs to an upper room, and we did bending and stretching. We sang some beautiful prayers in Sanskrit that rang a bell inside of me, ancient sounds that were reverberating in my soul. At the end of the yoga session, we did a deep relaxation, relaxing all the different parts of the body. I was transported. I said to myself, "This is *it*." Yoga and deep relaxation brought just the elixir I needed for my pain.

I'd been looking for my path in English literature. I had

read the Romantic poets, Wordsworth and Coleridge, Keats, Yeats; I'd read Shakespeare and Chaucer, wanting them to show me the path of the heart. Finally I found my own way. It was miraculous for me, a total change of my life. I began to do yoga and meditate regularly.

In 1971, I went to a yoga retreat with Swami Satchidananda. In those early days, it was quite an awe-inspiring experience—as well as rigorous. We had three days, much of which was in silence, something I'd never done before. It was amazing to experience that silence. I heard the sound of "Om" coming from the hills. I knew I wasn't imagining it. I knew that the earth makes sounds that all of us in our busy-ness can't hear. I was listening and I was hearing. I did walking meditations, yoga, and *seva* or service, and I kept it all in a journal. I made a pact with myself to meditate every day, and I've continued to keep my vow.

Later in a seminar, I went inside my inner mind and saw pictures about my life, my family, my childhood, and I was able to expand my consciousness. I was able to heal my relationship with my parents, where I saw them as beings who were on the wheel of life, working out their issues on this earth. I saw myself walking hand-in-hand with my daughter, and I said, "No, we need to be separate individuals and together at the same time." And so I saw her near me as I was walking down the beach. She was walking near me—strong, separate, yet together.

In the '70s, I attended numerous workshops and did more and more meditation. I met teachers from all over the world. I met the Karmapa, the Dalai Lama, Kalu Rimpoche, Ram Dass, Sufi teachers, Buddhist masters—to mention just a few. By 1974, another friend introduced me to Swami Muktananda from India. I didn't know too much about what he was doing, and I was reluctant to bow in front of him, as everyone was doing. But I finally did. Someone had told me, "When you bow in front of a great person, you're bowing to yourself. You're not bowing down to any idol. You're bowing to the Self." So when I bowed down in front of Muktananda, he hit me gently on the back with some peacock feathers. When I went to sit down, immediately, my body started shaking, and I began doing yogic breathing, called *pranayama*, quite involuntarily. I went into a profound state of meditation. I felt like a blanket of peace had been thrown around my entire body. It was truly deep. I said to myself, "My God, this is real!" For the next ten years on and off, I meditated, chanted, and studied with Muktananda—not directly with him all that time, but often in his presence. I also lived across the street from his ashram for six years. I did chanting every morning and taught programs on the *Bhagavad Gita* and on meditation.

Before that, living in Marin County, I had worked at an office of an eye doctor. He was an iridologist who read the iris of the eyes to see what might be going on in the body. It was an amazing time. In the '70s, all kinds of spiritual people came to this health office: Sufis, Buddhists, Hindus, yogis, writers, poets, meditators of all kinds came to have the irises of their eyes read and their eyesight checked, and I interviewed all of them. I met roshis, masters, monks and gurus. All of them came there, and it was a great education.

In the early '70s, I began teaching my own classes. I taught a class at Holistic Life University called "Visualization Healing." I also taught yoga, meditation, and workshops, such as "Journey to the Center of the Self." I also began doing one-on-one sessions with people, taking them deeply inside, helping them to get in touch with their difficulties, coming to understand and release them and then to transform their awareness. I called this work "inner healing." Not until 1987 did I find out that the work I did was also called "hypnotherapy."

Before this, I struggled greatly trying to find my way. I tried many different jobs. I sold cars, aloe vera juice, worked as a headhunter, worked at temp jobs in banks and answered phones in companies. I taught Evelyn Wood Reading Dynamics. I taught in a business college in East Oakland, and I worked in the eye doctor's office.

I had moved to Bolinas, a village on the Pacific coast. It was beautiful—for me, isolated but beautiful. I would do two hours of yoga a day, standing on my head and going into the lotus posture. I taught yoga. I wrote in my journals and made some beautiful cloisonné jewelry. My daughter loved the wildflowers of the countryside. She knew the names of every one. At one point, my daughter and I had nowhere to go, so we both agreed that we'd pitch two tents there for a while. It seemed like a great adventure; yet in some ways I felt fearful. It was beginning to rain, and the nights were so dark. This was another time of great inner transformation, and I learned to have faith. I continued to do a lot of yoga, threw the *I Ching*, learned to deal with the sow bugs and to keep ourselves dry. One day, at the Renaissance Faire, a wandering minstrel came up to me, looked me in the eyes, and recited a haiku. He said, "Since my house burned down, now I have a better view of the rising moon." My eyes filled with tears, moved not only by the words, but also by their synchronicity. I marveled that he had come directly to me with this wisdom.

After a time, my daughter and I found shelter, and soon after that we moved from Bolinas to Fairfax, where we lived for about four years. In Fairfax, we lived in a house with a huge living room. I had a partner who was a spiritual patron of the arts. He and I gave concerts almost every month—the Nubian oud player, Hamza El Din, kathak dancers from India, bamboo flute from Sachdev, shakuhachi music, and many more. I also taught yoga classes in that huge living room, where I continued to give workshops and individual sessions.

It was time to leave that place too, and I moved to Oakland to be near the ashram. I wanted to dive more fully into my *sadhana*, my spiritual practice, so every day I went there to chant and meditate—mornings and evenings. This was all wonderful; yet still my life was a struggle to make a living. I had no idea yet that I could get a certificate for the work I did with inner healing and actually make a living. I was aware that I was truly "underemployed." I prayed and I prayed. I wrote to Muktananda. I said, "Baba, my spiritual life is going so very well. I have these beautiful visions, but the rest of my life is so very difficult." And he wrote back to me, and he said, "It's wonderful that your spiritual life is going so very well. About the other part of your life—these things happen sometimes, but with your faith and your devotion, your life will be transformed." That became my mantra—that with my faith and my devotion, my life was being transformed. And so it was, step by step. This, in truth, is the essence of the lesson I was learning: to have faith in and devotion to the universe, no matter what the vicissitudes of life might be.

At a gathering one day, I met a woman, and she told me that she'd become certified as a hypnotherapist. "Well," I said to her, "What did you learn there?" She told me what she'd learned, and I said, "That's what I do!" And I now knew I could prosper doing this kind of work. I knew I could take this work for which I had deep passion, and have it become my career. So I became a certified hypnotherapist in 1987. I started giving free hypnosis demonstrations every Friday night in Berkeley. Sometimes one person would come—and sometimes ten. I'd tell them what I did and show them, and I'd sell some tapes, and it began to grow from there.

In 1984, I had moved away from the ashram, from Oakland to a tiny cottage in Berkeley. It was time to go. Baba had died, and my inner voice told me to just move along. My tiny cottage was to become not only my home, but also my hypnotherapy office. When clients came in, I moved two kitchen chairs together, facing one another, for the first part of our session. When we were ready to do deep relaxation, my own futon became the "couch." As rudimentary as it was, it was the beginning of something that was to grow much larger.

Leaving the ashram community became for me an experience of great deepening. Where I had at first wanted to simply shine the light on the difficulties of life and try to make them vanish, now my path was telling me: "Go through the dark forest instead of around or above it. There are rich experiences there. You will come to understand more about the depths of human experience. Then you can release and transform that experience and come into the light. The way out is through." I listened to this inner voice, and I allowed myself to pay close attention to the darkness, to allow its deep experience. I deepened and I grew. As I understood more and more fully that "the way out is through," the world of healing began to take on depth and form. I learned and incorporated many healing tools.

I thought it might be a good idea to go back to graduate school. I went to JFK University in Orinda in the Transpersonal Psychology program. I made some good connections there, but I found out after one year that it wasn't the direct route to my destiny. I knew my path was about healing, not psychology; it was about a special kind of ancient consciousness transformation that I knew I must pursue. So once again, I left the halls of ivy, and I dove more and more deeply into the world of healing.

Still growing in my work, I moved from my cottage to a larger place, and I was able to stretch out, in more ways than one. As my work grew, I began to give talks at conferences, first at the American Association of Hypnotist Examiners, and then at the National Guild of Hypnotists. I taught in another hypnotherapy school. I taught workshops in the extracurricular program at UC San Francisco. I began to go on the radio. I learned the art of public communication. Fortunately I was in a field that gave me all the tools I needed to work on myself. In 1991, after the completion of another relationship, I needed to dive into a major project, a book. I wrote *Healing is Remembering Who You Are: A Guide for Healing Your Mind, Your Emotions, and Your Life*. This was quite a project, as I learned about the world of publishing. The book later went through another printing, and then a publisher picked it up. This book project was for me the beginning of a fulfillment of a prophecy and dream. In the '70s, Baba's astrologer, Chakrapani, had read my astrological chart and told me I'd be an internationally known speaker and writer. I was very far from it at the time, but his words echoed in my head. It somehow kept ringing in my ears. I was to keep plodding on with my temp jobs and my struggles, perfecting my work and growing in my own strength and consciousness before anything would truly materialize.

I kept on teaching. I took people to retreats on the sacred mountain, Mount Shasta for four years—and to Kauai. My individual practice began to grow. I began to get more comfortable on the media, on radio and TV. I did a lot of writing—regular articles for the "Journal of Hypnotism"—and a new book, which I re-wrote about four times in different forms with different titles.

I came to an understanding of inner healing as a process of experiencing, releasing and transforming the difficulties of life. I share this knowledge with you in this book. I understood the need for us to know and explore the darkness, as its purpose is to instruct us. This art of paying attention to the difficulties became an important ingredient in the work—as well as the next two steps of releasing and transforming into higher understanding.

I began to teach workshops for a number of years in this, what I found to be my area of specialization, Transformational Healing. Gradually this developed into a school. I learned that I needed to be state licensed, and the process was arduous. The school and I both began to grow. We first held our classes in my living room in Oakland. Now I had a living room with two walls of glass. It overlooked Lake Merritt and had a balcony around both walls, with a beautiful garden filled with Quan Yins and Buddhas. After a while, we moved our training to the Berkeley Conference Center, and then, after they announced to us that they had to retrofit the building for earthquakes, we moved to our own center near Lake Merritt in Oakland.

Here I was on this train of destiny, taking this ride, moving from one station to another—sometimes staying a long time at a station, sometimes needing to move more quickly. Then a new gift came into my life.

In 1995, I met Ammachi—or Mata Amritanandamayi Devi—from India. She'd been described as an incarnation of the Divine Mother, and I'd heard she had an intoxicating presence. My curiosity led me to visit her.

When I went up to greet her, she whispered mantras in my ears, and my heart poured open. I knew I was in the presence of a divine goddess. Ammachi became a great inspiration to me. Her radiance inspires the flow of love.

Another gift came in the form of Mark Douglas. He had heard me give a talk at the National Guild of Hypnotists in Nashua, New Hampshire, and he came to California to attend our training. One day, he said to me, "Marilyn, I'd like to show you a new technique." At that time, I felt I had so many techniques that I didn't know what I'd do with one more, but he said to me, "This one is miraculous." I couldn't resist the miraculous, so Mark began to show me a tapping technique that he said could work to heal just about anything. I found that it truly did have healing powers and that I could combine it with the work I was doing. New doors opened, as this proved to be immensely popular and effective. Mark also introduced me to new technologies and gave me some equipment for my office that put me on the "information superhighway" in much larger ways.

I explain this effective tapping technique in detail in this book. Like a perfect puzzle piece it fits perfectly with transformational healing to create a healing approach of great power.

As you read this book, I do wish you a profound and meaningful journey. There is a lot of material here. You can read it all at once or in parts. You can use it not only to inspire you, but as a handbook for transformation.

It is given to you with great love.

Part Two

From Darkness into Light:

Transformational Healing

Transformational Healing is a movement from darkness into light.

Transformational Healing is a movement of consciousness through the difficulties of our lives and into advanced states of being in which miraculous shifts occur. Everyone is suffering in one way or another. The Vietnamese Buddhist monk, Thich Nhat Hanh, saw people who lost their arms and legs from mine fields, boat people who'd been raped and killed, and then he saw others in French cafes sipping coffee without a thought about the rest of the world. He vowed never to live a superficial life again. He was able, then, to transform the suffering he saw into wholeness and advanced states of awareness.

The very fact that most of us do not remember our higher consciousness and we identify with a limited reality, is a form of suffering. Impermanence is a form of suffering, too, and it is something that everyone must experience at one time or another. Everything on the earth plane is shifting incessantly—including the people we hold dear, our body parts, our homes, our incomes, and our possessions. And because everything is in flux, we are wise to go more deeply to a place of essence within, in which there is a sense of comfort in being "home," in being in a place of profound connection with a changeless level of serenity and truth.

Transformational Healing is a way of paying attention

to our suffering, looking at it from the witness state, experiencing how it feels or sounds or what it looks like, and then releasing and healing it by making this connection with a more transcendent state of consciousness. This helps us to view our difficulties differently by shifting our level of awareness. There is truly a temple of healing that exists within. The healing process is a movement from darkness into light, from the unreal to the real, and from death into immortality.

We can also understand that human suffering has value and even beauty. If you look at the panorama of human experience, you can see that it is a part of a range of highly valuable experiences that deepen and enrich the soul. It not only deepens, but it creates courage and strength. The daily frustrations, losses and insufficiencies—all of these are prods to push us on an upward path of spiritual awakening. There is a perfection to all things—even the most gross of human experiences in wars, terrorism, in acts committed against us. They are hard to bear, but something is being shifted around. Hearts are being deepened in their sorrow. Wounds, once opened, create opportunities to bring in grace and uplifted understanding.

Glaciers form, ice floes melt, mountains shift, volcanoes erupt, flowers die, species are born, predators leap, prey runs away—and everything happens in a natural flow of experience. It is both a horror show and a display of ecstasy. In the panoramic overview, it is the natural movement of things creating the unfoldment of life as we know it.

If we are able to experience our difficulties, allow ourselves to come to know and feel them, we can then move beyond them and come into the ultimate healing states.

Most of us know the story of Beauty and the Beast. Beauty has to live in the castle with the Beast—and at first she is terrified of him. The angry Beast roars and rages, but Beauty doesn't run away from him. She begins to find great value in him, and ultimately, she falls in love with him. In that process, the spell is broken, and the Beast becomes a prince.

The Beast is, of course, the darkness—the shadow element within. It is anger, fear, abuse that has been received or given, feelings of intimidation or lack of self-worth. This darkness is often very difficult to acknowledge.

Yet, in a moment of courage and awakening, you invite that shadow, that beast, to come out into the open to be acknowledged and understood. In doing so, the beast ceases to roar. Through awareness, compassion and the power of love, its very nature is transformed.

When this darkness is lurking in the corners of our being, it shows up as headaches, sickness, unresolved fear or anger—clouds covering our light. The moment these elements are acknowledged and even loved (because they are all extraordinary teachers), then you open up to the process of great transformation. At that point, the beast isn't the same anymore. It has been transformed.

The three stages of healing are:
experience, release, and transform.

The first phase of this healing work is allowing yourself to fully experience your experience, to come to know what's inside. The second is to release the experience, and the third is to transform it.

Every experience carries a richness and has value. Paying close attention is the first step in the process of self-knowledge. It is a process of looking with an inner microscope or magnifying glass and just seeing what's there. It's about looking, for example, at current experiences that are taking place in the body—pains, constrictions, tingling, holding—whatever is happening in the moment. It's also about looking at the mind and emotions—seeing whether there is sadness or rage or tightness or shame. It's about looking even more deeply at the experience, possibly finding the roots. The roots may be in childhood, or they may go all the way back to the womb. Or they may go to another lifetime, or to a belief or a tendency of the mind. We will look more deeply into these root causes later.

A woman named Anne had been feeling anxiety, turmoil and confusion in herself for years. She had no idea why, until one day when the doors inside of her consciousness opened. In deep relaxation, she saw a scene that took place when she was six. She was standing on a curb with her brother, and a car was turning a corner right near them. She tried to step back and bring her little brother back with her—but she couldn't. She had always felt that she was the cause of her little brother's death from this car. She now saw something stored deeply within her subconscious mind. There was someone else there—an older man behind her little brother, and he was not stepping back. None of them could move because this man was not stepping back, and the child was killed.

Anne began to cry, "My God—we can't step back because there's that man there! I didn't cause my brother's death!" She was shifted profoundly at this moment, as years of tension floated up and off her body and mind. As she sobbed, her body and mind entered a state of very deep relaxation. This changed her life, as she could now grieve her brother's death and know that she was not the cause.

By allowing herself to experience the emotions that were causing her such distress in her life, she was led deeply into their roots, and she was able to experience a revelation that altered the course of her life. In similar ways, you can explore pain, old traumas, tendencies of the mind, fragments of self, and the exploration will lead you to some form of self-knowledge that can create more freedom within you. A transformational experience is often embedded in the experiencing process.

Not only does the deep inner mind function as a repository of all the records of past experiences, but it also miraculously stores solutions—innate homeopathic remedies of the soul, gifted to us to solve the dilemmas of our lives. Within the memory banks of the subconscious lie images, metaphors, flashes of wisdom, healing directives that the ancient Greeks and Romans knew how to tap in their healing temples. The solutions essentially lie within the soul.

A woman named Joan had been married for many years to a man who'd left her—suddenly and for another woman. This was a shock to her whole being. For a while, she couldn't function, but finally she went back to graduate school. Still, she found herself biting her nails and gritting her teeth, being easily distracted and not thinking clearly. She knew that something in her subconscious was using up her energy.

In deep relaxation, her mind went to an empty warehouse. She was there alone, and it was dark. She sat down on the floor, as there was no furniture. Her dog was there with her—and though she loved her dog, she felt sad because it was not a human being that was near her. She felt her aloneness, her anger and her grief.

Next, amazingly, something came into this picture that calmed her completely. She saw a blue light that was profoundly comforting. She had no idea that great spiritual teachers have called the "blue light" the color of consciousness itself. The blue light underlies all matter in the universe and can be seen in the center of a flame. Seeing this light within brought great peace to her.

Then she went to a pond of water, which she instinctively knew was healing water. At first, she began to sink, "like Hamlet's Ophelia," she said.

But she didn't sink completely like Ophelia did. Something was buoying her up—and she was floating!

She knew from her own intrinsic imagery that she'd make it and that all was well. Darkness had become light; sinking became floating. She could even stop biting her nails because she was allowing herself to experience her feelings and their roots. Actually, she'd been "eating herself up" inside and outside—quite literally. Now she had no need to do that anymore. She now has the knowledge that she is moving to the other side of her darkness.

Release is a clearing out that initiates an opening of a reality that had been closed or unknown.

Sometimes release happens naturally as a direct result of "looking deeply" or "paying attention." Other times, we can assist in the release process by using techniques such as energy therapy, which taps away old traumas, fears, resentments, guilt, grief, shame, anger and emotional trauma. You can find a variety of release techniques in part 6 of this book.

Release is a clearing out of your consciousness. It's like cleaning out your closets and drawers, releasing old correspondence or outworn clothes. As you discard these, you ready yourself to invite in a new level of your life. You're ready to initiate an opening of a reality that had previously been either closed or unknown.

Release, again, often takes place as a natural outgrowth

of paying attention to your experience, like Joan did when she saw the blue light. As you stay with your experience, often a miracle happens. One person found a lotus at the bottom of a murky pond. Another felt as if she were experiencing a birth process through a very dark tunnel and out into an experience of light.

Another way to experience the transcendent is to call it forth. You may call in a guide to assist you; you may surround yourself with light—or beam it on your previous difficulties; you may bring love and comfort to your past, present and future; you may feel the presence of a transcendent figure or consciousness that shifts your situation into another dimension of light, joy, awareness, love and peace.

A woman named Karen had been fearful all her life. She looked deeply at her fear one day and saw it symbolically. She was a mother wolf devouring her young cubs ferociously. She cried when she discovered this, cried when she found this dark and predatory nature in her own self. She was like the Goddess Kali with skulls all around her, and she was battling the dark forces inside of herself. Did she fear her own ferocious power? Just seeing this made her weep with the recognition of her power. Now she found herself able to accept it. No more would she have to rely only on the mace and whistle she carried on her keychain. She knew she was a goddess of both darkness and of light.

As we have said, very often the way to the light is through the difficulty. It is about diving into the full experience of the dual universe—the dark and light, the sacred and profane, the sensitive and gross—and moving into knowledge, love and profound inner power.

By moving into these altered dimensions, you find perceptual shifts in which you see everything in your life from a new perspective. It may mean, for example that you see everything that has happened to you as a kind of blessing to help you become a wiser, more compassionate human being. It may mean that you see someone who's hurt you as a powerful agent of change in your life and who has perhaps propelled you to seek higher ground.

You come to understand the trials of your life as transformational experiences.

In addition to perceptual shifts, you also find that you understand the life of the spirit with greater depth. As you move through darkness and into the light, you come to understand the trials of your life as transformational experiences. Something then lifts from you and lightens your load. You feel it emotionally, physically and spiritually. You are lifted into lighter emotions. Your electrical and biochemical systems are moved into states of well being. You are lifted up spiritually so that you understand experientially that there is a source of great power that lives within you. This is the nature of transformation.

William Blake knew about this when he so

nonchalantly began one of his poems with the line, "As I was walking amongst the fires of hell one day...." He knew he could walk there because he was going to walk right out to the other side into levels of consciousness in which he could "see heaven in a wildflower and eternity in an hour."

Exploring the darkness can ultimately lift you into a more infinite reality in which you are in touch with your essence. As you combine this process with the shifting of the electromagnetic energy system, you provide even more avenues for change.

As you read on, you'll understand more fully the root causes of your current challenges, how to find them, and how to move through them into expanded levels of consciousness. We are working, as you remember, with the subconscious, the higher self, the mind and the energy system. All of these are the components of a healing system that moves you gracefully from darkness into light.

By understanding the root causes of your difficulties, you can come to know a more enlightened level of life.

It's common in our culture to think that all problems stem from early childhood. One person even went so far as to say that being born into a particular family or culture is as if we were abducted at birth by aliens and were brainwashed by their cult. And though it's really significant to consider how we were formed in our early lives, understanding the root causes of what makes us the way we are goes much deeper than that.

The true primal cause of what ails us, no matter what our early lives were like, is the sense of separation that most humans feel at one time or another. It's not being connected to the essence of things. It's like being thrown out of the Garden of Eden, out of the harmony, out of the oneness—thrown almost rudely into a feeling of separation or desolation. These are human feelings, and they come from being in the illusion of isolation rather than in the state of unity. Life on earth is a journey back to the center, back home to the essence of the soul. Being away from it is the chief cause of our difficulties.

With separation as the bottom line, there are still other reasons why we suffer. There are very important issues of childhood and parents—but it is not quite so simple; the root causes run deep.

Samskaras and *vasanas* are tendencies of the mind that we bring here with us. They come with our birth certificate and are built into us. They can be from past lives. It's common in our culture to view babies as innocent creatures; yet babies bring thought forms and tendencies with them at birth. We already have *samskaras* in our beings when we come into this world, and these constitute the issues that we come here to work out.

What we then do is to magnetize to ourselves in our lifetimes, specific incidents that will bring forth our innate *samskaras*. So we don't "get" our problems from our parents. We magnetize a particular kind of parent or situation into our lives so that we can work out the issue. These issues come up in order for us to heal them. We need to have them brought forth in a strong way in order for us to get the point. We're here to heal. So we have parents and boyfriends and girlfriends, husbands and cousins, and sicknesses and work situations in order to bring forth our *samskaras,* so that we can heal them. We are by nature electromagnetic. We're vibrating electrically and magnetically, so we draw things to us according to the nature of our thought forms. Within us are inborn *samskaras,* and we draw to us these situations that are karmic. It seems that our destiny has to do with our *samskaras* that we are here to heal. Let's just say that we're "working out our stuff." *Samskaras* equal "stuff" that most likely has origins in other lifetimes. For those who don't believe in other lifetimes, it's okay. You can interpret them as concurrent realities, the collective unconscious, or metaphors. They don't have to be literal past lives— though many people believe that we have incarnated many times. And not only have we incarnated, but we've also been accumulating wisdom. That's the whole *raison d'être* for our lives—that what we're here to do is heal the issues of our egos so that we can lift our consciousness up and move on to other levels of growth.

So all of our issues do not stem from "parents." The roots of our suffering are panoramic. The roots are in our consciousness.

So, given the fundamental root causes of separation and *samskaras,* there are other areas in which these issues manifest. Here are some of them:

- Problems stemming from the womb

- Issues from the birth experience

- Wounds that we pick up that belong to others—parents, teachers, peers

- Incidents from past lives

- Difficulties with or from other souls who are affecting us

- Issues arising from our own subpersonalities

- Problems from core beliefs and ingrained patterns that are bred deeply into us and that form our comfort zones

- Traumatic experiences we've had

- Cultural and economic factors that serve as our contexts

- Our inherited tendencies and our *karmas*, which provide the lessons of our lifetimes

There are many factors that affect us, and they are all connected to the original illusion of separation from the essence of the soul. It is helpful to understand these root causes, for then we can release and heal them. We will be looking at these factors in greater detail.

Some people want to know why we have to dredge up this stuff. Why not just go to the light and shine it on ourselves or just "be healed"? I used to believe this myself, but I found that diving deeply into greater understanding, emerging and then soaring into the light was for me a more complete and enduring way to heal. What I have found to work is to move though one issue after another in a lifelong healing process, find the areas of difficulty and move through them until they are transformed into ecstasy and enlightenment.

For this we use the deep inner healing processes and the energy therapy that we've been talking about. When we relax enough to get to the deep material, we allow the conscious mind to let go of its barriers, the guardians at the gates, so that the inner material is revealed. The material of healing from higher consciousness is then revealed as well. You'll find full directions on how to do this in part 6.

One of the deepest root causes of suffering is our attachment to things staying the same.

One of the Buddha's Noble Truths is the necessity of ultimately overcoming our attachment to things staying the same. Buddha called this attachment a primary cause of our suffering. We expect everything to stay the same, even though the fundamental law of the material plane is change. We expect that our mates, families, finances, material environments, governments will be the way we expect them to be, the way we've grown used to them. Yet everything is a part of a third dimensional universe in which the law of flux and change is in constant operation. Because of change, we experience loss, grief and separation, until we learn to flow gracefully with the inevitable changes of life. This doesn't mean that we can't grieve our losses. It means that in order to heal, we can first grieve and then we can step back enough to align ourselves with the laws of change, so that we can move to whatever the next step might be. Singer Julie Andrews, after an illustrious singing career, lost her voice. After grieving, she is given the challenge of seeing what else might be in store for her in this next phase of her life. Christopher Reeve was given the challenge of releasing his attachment to moving his physical body when he was paralyzed. He was given an opportunity to make a leap into another level of consciousness.

Lifelong impressions are created in the womb and at birth.

Not only is the infant state important, but so is the state of the fetus. Prenatal and perinatal (actual birth) experiences are also, for many people, at the core of our present difficulties. The times of gestation and entrance into the third-dimensional world can be keys to current issues. Messages, thought forms, emotions, deep internal experiences are being sent biochemically and electromagnetically from the mother to the fetus. *In utero,* a great deal of material of all sorts is being passed back and forth. When you heal these states, you can go back to see what might have been going on in the psyche of the mother and in the fetus. Some people find their mother to have been in a state of trauma during her pregnancy. Others find that she didn't really want to have a child at that time. Still others find that their mother was at peace all the way through her pregnancy. Fetuses pick up these flows of experience energetically and biochemically, and you can often bring great awareness and healing to these experiences by returning to the womb through deep relaxation techniques. Imagine for example that you or a client has a feeling of abandonment. You might go back to the womb where the mother might have been getting ready to have an abortion. And you as a soul would tune into the vibration of that mother. Imagine you're inside the body of a person for almost a year.

Although you do have *samskaras*, impressions that you bring with you, you are also in a womb environment that exacerbates them. In the womb are body fluids, thought forms, and emotions, and you are profoundly influenced by this environment. If your parents were fighting all the time—of if your mother was unhappy or getting divorced, if there was a death that happened in the family right at that time, you might take on all this grief. Abandonment is, of course, an issue that essentially arises because of lack of connection with Source. It can be healed, nevertheless, by looking at any part of yourself. Since we are holographic, in that each part of us carries the whole within us, you can look for awareness and healing by revisiting the experiences of the womb—as well as in the present moment.

There are also root causes of our current predicaments in the birth experience. Sometimes the birth is very difficult. Perhaps there were forceps used. Perhaps there was a c-section. Some c-section children feel that they need help. They can't do things themselves. The birth process, is of course, most profound—the undulations and the physical experiences of the body moving through the birth canal, the biochemicals present, all are important to later development. One little boy born by c-section was constantly saying to his mother "I need help, Mommy." This is, of course, his *samskara*—not because of the birth. He brings that to this lifetime and needs that situation in order to exacerbate the *samskara*, so that ultimately he can heal it.

In a healing situation, if you find a lack of love in that womb or birth experience, you can bring profound awareness there. You can be a vehicle for the presence of healing love. You can create a rebirth experience. You can bring an experience of light or enlightenment to the fetus or the baby.

You can take a look to see if any current images that might come forth in the healing process are birth images. One woman felt as if she were in a tunnel, and she saw light at the end. She knew that this also symbolized that she was going through some very difficult life situations as well, and she was ready to see the light in the experiences of her life.

You can also do some energy therapy by tapping on any traumatic experiences that may still remain. It's important to remember that no matter what the womb or birth experience may be, we are still bringing our own issues there, our own *samskaras*, to be re-experienced and healed. There is, therefore, no blame, and it all provides a perfect opportunity to heal.

Other root causes of our challenges are from experiences in infancy.

My mother told me that once, when I was a baby, I cried all night. She usually picked me up at night, but the neighbors told her that one particular time, her baby cried all night. My mother had been so tired from getting up every night that she didn't hear me cry. I had felt within me that some kind of abandonment had taken place, even though I knew that my mother hadn't really abandoned me.

I just knew that crying all night long was some kind of core experience for me. If you really get a sense of what infancy is like, you can see the root causes of so many of our adult dilemmas. Imagine the comfort of being held in someone's arms, being held up to someone's breast, being stroked, experiencing a primal feeling of being cared for totally. These are the idyllic situations we look for in drugs, food, and the ceaseless striving for satisfaction in relationships. These states are profoundly connected with infancy. They are attempts to reclaim (and for some to find for the first time) this primal comfort. They are graphic examples of the root causes of what ails us in our adult lives.

Past life events are opportunities for healing and awakening.

Whether you consider past lives real or metaphoric— or as concurrent realities or experiences of the collective unconscious, there is great healing in exploring and transforming them.

Just like every current event in our lives, every past life event is an opportunity for healing and awakening. Understanding our past lives can help us to go into some of the deepest causes of our current predicaments. In our past lives, we can also come to meet inner fragments of ourselves that have been living in darkness. The material that lies in our psyches consists of freeze-frames, some of which are pictures of unresolved traumas and our deepest emotions. We can experience, release and transform these and bring significant healing to our lives.

Healing our past lives is about shining the light of consciousness on the difficult places so that they become transformed within us. No longer is our past life self, that ancient man or woman freeze-framed in our consciousness, all alone somewhere in a forgotten land. When we bring love and healing to these situations, great transformation is possible. Our soul learns from and transcends all the past difficulties, and this heals the way we carry the old wounds within us.

A woman named Shirley went to a past life in which she was a man, a barbaric medieval warrior. After a day's work was done, they'd go to a big table in a mead hall. They'd get some large ham shanks and chow down. You can get the picture of this burly grunting warrior, after the day's warring was over, sitting at the huge wooden table and devouring the meat. He had a raw kind of power, and he was, as we found out, a precursor to her tendency to "chow down" after going to work every day, going to her own kinds of "wars" in the business world. She'd felt extremely guilty about overeating, and she'd gained a lot of weight coming home and sitting there, gobbling food after work. But after seeing the root cause, seeing the past life prototype, she had a great awakening, and she was able to use the tapping process instead of overeating to work with such inner states as "feeling weakened by the world" or "feeling frustrated" or "feeling drained by work" or "needing sustenance." She was able to make a great transformation when she worked directly with her feelings rather than obscuring them with food.

Other people with food issues go to past lives in which they have starved. Some with throat problems have gone to past life experiences of forced oral sex or of traumas from not having had enough food. In your mind's eye, you can heal the traumas, bring in love where the wounds used to be, tap on the meridians, and there is a return to wholeness.

One woman said that she'd been taught that all your problems go back to your parents, and she said "but I know that I set my parents up because of the past life experiences I had."

A man named Dan suffered from acute claustrophobia. He knew he soon had to fly on a plane, and he was beginning to panic. In order to understand the roots of this, in a session, he went back to a past life in England in 1905. He worked in a newspaper and tobacco shop, and he went down some stairs to a lower room that had a trap door. A fire broke out, and he was unable to get out, so he suffocated in the fire. He deeply felt the trauma of this experience, and he was able to both experience and release it. By releasing it; he was able to imagine enclosed spaces that are cozy, like a womb when it is comfortable, and to realize that he could now fly on airplanes because the past life experience was over. It was complete, and he could now let it go.

One of the great transformational tools we have is the ability to stand back and look at events from a state of *witness consciousness*; this gives us a wise eye and an expanded perspective. This "witness" is our true self. When we see from this perspective, we are able to ask, "What was I learning in this past life? What is the value in this trauma or event for my soul? What am I learning now?" There is invariably an emotional thread running through our past lives to the present—moving us toward healing the thread of our *samskaras*, the deep emotional and mental impressions that dwell in our souls from lifetime to lifetime. The grief that we carry, the tendency to feel afraid of speaking our truths, the tendency to feel slighted or rejected or hurt or angry or terrified—these are tendencies that dwell in our souls in lifetime after lifetime of freeze-frames that have gone unhealed. And the purpose of our re-experiencing them over and over again is to heal them, to come to terms with them, to set ourselves free through a transformation of consciousness.

If you look for a thread of a *samskara* in your life, you may first find a current dominant thought pattern. Then you might take it back as far as you can—perhaps to roots in past lives. There is a deep core of emotional truth as you allow yourself to experience this root. To remove it is like extracting a sliver from the soul, and then healing takes place.

In some of my own past life experiences is the thread of abandonment. I've mentioned my experience in this lifetime as an infant who once cried all night, with a sleeping mother who was too tired to hear me. My crying with no one coming left a mark upon me. I go back farther, and I'm a Native American woman, left alone in an embankment of snow to die. There's a man standing there—and he turns and walks away.

I go back even further, and I'm an Asian woman, bereft and anguished because my children have been killed in a fire. Back further, and I'm standing on the bow of a ship somewhere, once again bereft and terrified because my husband has drowned on the tumultuous seas.

By invoking my connection with the power of healing, I ask to see the transformation of these events. I see the Native American woman's soul rise up out of the embankment of snow, surrounded in light. I realize that the true way of seeing this, from the point of view of the soul, is that she is in no way left alone to freeze and rot in the snow. Her soul shines through and ascends. I know that any time, any moment, I can call for the elevation of my own consciousness so that I can see with the eyes of the soul.

In the same way, the Asian woman (me), in her grief at the loss of her children, has been given the fullness of heart to love all the children of the universe. She is embraced by divine compassion. The same for the woman whose husband has died at sea. After the full experience of this grief and loss, and after some experiences of release, she is moved to a state of comfort and oneness on the level of the soul.

This is the divine art of consciousness transformation, which can happen in a flash of a moment, and can change the entire outlook of our lives. Even though we set ourselves free at one moment doesn't necessarily mean that we set ourselves free the next. We have to keep working on it, keep at it, keep on remembering the transformational work we came here for—and keep on bringing the light to every aspect of ourselves.

This inner work is about going to the deepest roots of our suffering, stirring the pot and bringing them to the surface, shining the light of consciousness upon them, thereby transforming them and bringing greater freedom to the soul. This is the work we came here to do, the great healing of our lives.

Early traumas can leave powerful marks.

When we look at what is holding people back in their lives, keeping them from self-realization, one of the most important factors is trauma. Some people have been traumatized early in life, but trauma can happen at any time. People who've been traumatized often go into shock, and the shock has left them with an inner picture, a freeze-frame, an almost catatonic part of the self that still exists inside. What happens is that this part of the self draws to it pain and suffering and sometimes even similar events. We are electromagnetic, and we draw to ourselves, like magnets, what is reflected from within. Our beings are also seeking to heal themselves, so traumas and other experiences keep showing themselves to us in an effort to be healed.

You can make powerful shifts in these traumatic experiences, and you'll find specific techniques for this in parts 6 and 7.

It is always helpful to ask yourself what this difficulty has done to evolve you. How has it contributed to the growth and evolution of your soul? How have you needed this in order to become the person that you are today? This is a very important question, because it's often very difficult to find a reason for our suffering. Everyone who's a healer (and most of us are in one way or another) has had great suffering. This phenomenon has been called the "wounded healer." You can look at your life as a tragedy;

yet it is also a school. You can come to understand that you're learning, evolving, growing into spiritual wisdom, and often this comes through trials. This shifts the whole context of how you perceive the events of your life. You make extraordinary inroads into the experience of the enlightened self.

One woman named Jeanette had intense pain throughout the left side of her body, from the top of her head to the bottoms of her feet. She walked with a three-pronged cane and with great difficulty. As she talked, her body was contracted in pain. She talked at length about the things she'd done to try to alleviate her pain—none of which had worked. She'd been to famous clinics and doctors to no avail. I asked her, "Have you ever been abused?" and she began to cry. She said, "I got married at age fifteen, and from that day on, my husband physically abused me and all the children. He beat us every single day." And she said, "And that's not all. There's more to the story." She paused and took a deep breath, and then she uttered the next three words: "I shot him." At this point, the bottom dropped out, and she was sobbing. So I said to her, "You know, you're carrying that guilt and pain around in your body." And she cried some more, because she knew that she had spoken the truth. So we did some healing. We brought healing to the part of her that had been wounded by calling upon the healing power of Jesus, as she was a Christian, and this worked for her. As Jesus touched her, the fragmented part of her soul was soothed. We did some energy therapy. We used actual balloons as she communicated with her deceased husband (see part

6), and she released his energy from her life. She held the balloon in her hands, exploding it as she let go of all her rage and grief. In two weeks, she returned smiling with high-heeled shoes on, ready to work on weight loss. Her profound traumas had been experienced, released and transformed.

Another woman named Karen had been date-raped. Although she had a very strong connection with her spiritual path, this trauma was a thorn in her psyche, and it had caused her to feel extraordinarily wounded, scattered, filled with shame. In herself, she knew that ultimately she wanted to see this all as an initiation and a deepening. She wanted to know how this could be a blessing, but the energy of weakness and shame pervaded her. Energy therapy helped her to decrease her feelings of shame, abandonment, lack of protection, inner panic and insecurity. She released the energy of the perpetrator from her psyche. She nurtured the traumatized part of herself. She made enormous shifts inside, and finally one day, she felt a sense of freedom. She felt a sense of relief that she could let it go and just be.

Traumas can be transformed by shifting the energy, by the light of healing and the power of love. All of us have experienced the *original trauma*, the pain of separation, being "cast out of the Garden of Eden," being away from home—out of Kansas, out of the Oneness with all that is. We have to deal with this and find out how to get back home. This is what we came to this earth to do. We also have to handle the myriad of other abandonments, rejections and traumas that the flesh and psyche are heir to. Fortunately we have the tools to do this, and we can bring our lives full circle back into the essence of ourselves in which we feel centered and clear.

Many people are carrying the wounds of their parents as their own.

We can receive these "soul scars" by early or even later programming, through genetics or as samskaras, tendencies of the mind carried through the generations. It is truly remindful of the Biblical discussion of the "sins of the fathers" being "visited upon the children." This is the root cause of a number of our difficulties.

It is not a way to shift responsibility, however; it is good to remember that ultimately we are all working out our own "stuff," and receiving it from some particular "donor" is a symptom, not a cause. Nevertheless, it is hard sometimes to find the immediate origins of some of our challenges, and we do have to look at parents' wounds for some answers.

A woman named Janet experienced sadness and depression that defied "rational" explanation. She did have difficulties with alcohol, and her boyfriend had broken up with her. She'd been experiencing bouts of total desolation. Sometimes she'd stay in bed all day and not go to work. So we looked at how her mother handled her own life. All her mother's life, she would lie down on the couch and remain immobile for hours when her husband would go out with other women. She'd be totally wiped out and thoroughly victimized. And though it might have been appropriate for Janet to experience emotional responses to her losses, her experiences were nevertheless more prolonged than they might have been had there not been these deeper issues involved. She had picked up her mother's response pattern; this had brought forth her own *samskara* or tendency of the mind.

Infants are also quite impressionable, even "psychic." They pick up emotions and deep psychological impressions from the world in which they live. One woman, in looking at her underlying depression that she could not explain, talked about the fact that when she was a child, her father was a classic couch potato. He did nothing but work, watch TV and grunt "hello" every once in a while. In addition to this woman's deep need for him to have given her more love, she also psychically felt in herself the depression that was his. Understanding this, we can then "release" her father's influence on her psyche and bring love to the young girl who was ignored.

Some parents have been actual victims of holocausts or great tragedies, and their offspring will inherit the legacy of victim consciousness, protracted sadness or terrifying thoughts. Sara's parents had been in concentration camps. She was troubled with frequent images of horror that came quite uninvited into her mind. We did some energy therapy on the horror pictures, on her despair, on her fear of pain, on her anxiety about life. We then reminded her that she was awakening to the fact that "life is but a dream" and that the "horror stories are over." When she went into a state of profound relaxation, she saw angels.

One was a paper cutout from an old-fashioned book. The other was resting on a huge down pillow. She felt protected and safe and comforted. The angels told her to rest, to take it easy, to let herself experience safety and feel the comfort. They told her that she'd been on a very scary ride, but that scary ride had come to an end. Sara found the sanctuary of the soul, in which there is peace and healing. We reminded her that she could watch from a state of *witness consciousness* and transform her reality with the power of truth.

This was a major breakthrough for Sara. Her thoughts became more positive. She also had tools to handle any difficult ones that might arise. She could watch them, transform them, tap on them or just let them go. She was now able to think about her work and how she wanted to become a speaker. She actually did this, and she began to give talks about ways of transforming your life.

Within us is a multiplicity of selves, called subpersonalities.

Most of us know that we are not one simple personality. There's the critical self, the prankster self, the rebellious self, the parental self, the procrastinator self, the priest or priestess self. There's one who wants to retreat and another who wishes to stand in the spotlight, one who is terrified and another who is fearless. The inner child is a subpersonality (as well as a "freeze frame" in the memory bank). So too are the inner teenager and the young adult.

One who comes up often is Poor Pitiful Pearl. That's the one who can't succeed, who sits desolate and alone with a babushka on her head, hands cupping her face. It's amazing how many people have subpersonality bag ladies and bag men inside of them.

So we go deeply inside to pay attention to these parts of self. We find out what they want or need and what function they're providing inside. Is she there to provide protection, to help someone stay within the appointed zones of comfort? We can talk to her and find out. We can help to release the subpersonalities or show them how to get their needs met in other ways.

The inner child is a very important subpersonality, and there are many other Jungian, mythological and other archetypes that have been found to be universal. It's very fruitful to find the ones that are intrinsic for each person. It's always enlightening to make contact with this important cast of characters that constitutes the self.

We all have tendencies of the mind and core beliefs.

Some people have a tendency to make everything catastrophic. Others idealize everything. Some have tendencies to be generous or greedy, cynical or optimistic, dominant or submissive, arrogant or self-deprecating. All of these tendencies come with the birth certificate. We've already talked of *samskaras*, tendencies of the mind that we're born with. Understanding this shows us that babies are not as innocent as we've been led to believe.

Some people have a tendency to create the "worst possible scenario" and worry that the cataclysm will happen any moment to destroy everything. Others live in the reality that the Golden Age of peace is upon us, and the lions and the lambs will soon lie down together.

These tendencies are connected with core beliefs. Some people feel they'll never be happy or that they're not worth anything, and these beliefs are root causes of key issues in their lives. One man's core belief was, "Nobody likes me." Because of this, he had a difficult time getting a date. At five years old, his mother took him to the train station and put him, his brother and his father on the train and said, "Goodbye, I'll see you sometime." And his mother didn't see him until he was twenty years old. This traumatic experience would certainly leave anyone with the notion that "Nobody likes me." There are those who take this back to origins in past lives, and it's often fruitful to search there for roots. To help him, we took him back to the scene in deep relaxation, and we brought in his adult self to love that boy. Then we explored with him his mother's psyche to understand what she had done. He needed to experience his anger and pain, and he was able to release them by understanding that this was his great life lesson; he could now feel more at peace by understanding that this was a pivotal moment in his life that set him on his path of healing.

When we see predicaments and wounds from expanded perspectives, we can understand them as the raw material for growth and enlightenment. Some understand them as lessons and blessings. When seen from an even more expanded perspective, they are the play of light and shadow, of expansion and limitation, on the panoramic backdrop of higher consciousness. They are very powerful "illusions" indeed.

There are other powerful root causes of our suffering.

There is a body of knowledge called "spirit release" or "entity release." It's based on the belief or experience that there are spirits that are attached to us and are causing our difficult behaviors and our suffering. Those who work in this area describe some of the spirits as earthbound entities, beings who have died, but who have not passed into other dimensions and are attached to living people as hosts. Some of the entities are described as "demonic," and this, to those who do this work, accounts for many of the transgressions and experiences of evil on earth. The work to release these "entities" consists of making contact with them and releasing them into the light.

There is also a great deal written about *karma* and destiny, which asserts that your suffering is preordained as a result of previous actions that you've taken in other times. A part of the healing process in this paradigm consists of creating shifts in attitudes around and acceptance of one's destiny. In this context, it may be that reframing your experiences, by understanding all the vicissitudes of your life as necessary for your growth, can be healing in itself.

There is another body of knowledge that considers the socioeconomic contexts in which we live. If you live in a war-torn political environment, for example, your life experience will differ from that of someone living in a relatively peaceful, stable and prosperous country. This dovetails with our understanding of karma and destiny, as well. You may want to look at how being born in Bosnia or Cambodia has created different experiences for your growth than being born in London or California.

There are also other powerful roots of our suffering. Physical issues, illnesses, pain and hunger are important roots. The emotional issues that come from misidentifying yourself as a being separate from your essence, your Source—all of these create states of human suffering.

When you return to a state of unity and understanding, experiences in which your heart is so open that you feel the all-pervasive love and peace at the core of all existence, this is when the veils lift, and suffering ceases.

In part 3 of this book, we'll be looking at this state of consciousness, which lies at the root of our healing. It lies at the root of our very being and is what we have all been put on earth to know.

Our preconceived paradigms create the experiences we have.

We magnetize our experiences to us both in our own lives and as healers. We experience what we consciously or unconsciously expect to experience. For example, when one woman takes people into deep regressions, most of them do Nostradamus predictions. Some people who do healing work expect that those who come to them will have emotional experiences. Some expect others to go to the beginning of time when the Big Bang took place and toxins were released. Or some people expect you to go to only the inner child or to past lives. What you have as your paradigm or your expectation is what happens. If you expect people to go to life between lives, then they will. You can call the phenomenon "psychic energy"—or "the airwaves" or "intention" or the "electromagnetic vibration" you're emitting. One researcher studied the different paradigms that various therapists and healers have for what they expect to happen in their sessions, and she found that they manifested exactly what they subconsciously expected to manifest.

As you read on, you'll enter the realm of higher consciousness, which is the inner remedy given to us as our birthright to heal all the root issues of our lives.

Part Three

Higher Consciousness:
The Next Dimensions of Healing

*The ultimate healing returns us to connection
with our infinite self.*

There is a meadow on Mt. Shasta called Panther
Meadow. If you follow a wildflower-lined stream up the
meadow, you come to a small hole with bubbles rising to
the surface. This is the source of the stream. From this, a
great flow of fresh water bubbles up from below and
pours down the mountain.

In the same way, great healing is about bringing
yourself back to the source of the most magnificent
healing from within. We've been wandering in the forest
of duality, through fear, anger, shame, grief, and guilt—and
now we're invited to return home. And even though these
states of duality are instructive, we are here to move
through and beyond them to the Source.

Healing, nevertheless, is the work of a lifetime. We
don't just "get healed" and that's that. We move through
layer after layer, visiting the healed states of love and
wisdom, sometimes having to venture out into our
difficulties again to learn a bit more about the nature of
limitation—until that day that we can reside exclusively
in the expanded state.

A very accomplished woman, a physician named Ann,
had a childhood in which she'd experienced many
abandonments. Emotional patterns of pain and sadness, of
being in a "black hole," remained with her. By consistently
paying careful attention to the abandoned girl she carried

within her, she was able to embrace her suffering enough to lift up the patterns. She had allowed herself to experience the pain of perceived abandonment and the fear that she'd live in that darkness forever. She felt love and compassion arise from a deep source, and she instantly understood that she'd been given this pain so that she could know what suffering was. She worked with suffering people every day, and she was able to help them because she knew their experience. She now could return to the enlightened, compassionate self that was her essence.

Healing such patterns of the mind brings us back to the sanctuary that resides in the soul. When we go on such excursions, we return to life with an altered point of view, and this inner connection transforms our suffering.

Here in part 3, we're paying attention to the states of higher consciousness that transform suffering. These inner healing states are: love, compassion, forgiveness, wisdom, witness consciousness, light and peace.

The greatest healing gift is love.

Healing love is a divine energy that is the supreme force for healing. It is the remedy that lifts us up out of limited awareness and transforms our old illusions of being separate from the universe. William Blake said, "And we are put on earth a little space/To learn to bear the beams of love." Every object, animate and inanimate, has within it living vibrations, dancing molecules that are composed of the energy of love. In actuality, all matter and energy are love, itself. This is a profound awareness, an invitation to awaken to an expanded level of being.

When you awaken to this awareness, you realize that you have the ability to consciously bring the beams of love, these outflows from the heart of all creation, to parts of self that have been hanging out in darkness for too long. This is how you're able to create in yourself a harmonious reunion of all segments of your being, bringing all disconnected fragments of yourself together in love.

This awareness transforms you. You feel a sense of elevation and amplified strength. When you experience the love vibration, you touch all parts of yourself, all fragments or subpersonalities, with the elixir of love. The results are stunning.

You can touch with love the child or infant or teen or past-life selves within or the critical or angry or unloved inner selves that are held as freeze-framed photos in the library of your consciousness. You can touch these parts with great kindness, compassion, and absolute divine love. This is how to help these wandering fragments of self to remember the love that's at the very heart of all creation, help them to remember they've been living in the illusion of suffering, and now it's time to return to the center of the heart.

Inner love is a healing elixir. It can be applied to negative mind states, sad parts of self, angry parts, parts from past lives who've been gravely mistreated or abandoned. It's an opportunity to bring great love to self-doubt, alienation and grief. We carry the love vibration in our aura, and it has the capability to surround and shift any negative vibration. When you take the time to pay attention to your difficulties, when you allow yourself to be present with them, the state of love naturally comes forth.

Love is a frequency band that changes the rate of vibration of everything it touches.

Love is an actual physical healing power because it speeds up the vibration and shifts the frequency of matter. When you experience old wounds and issues in this high frequency vibration, you shift your perception of these memories.

If you look inside at the infant that resides within you as a freeze-frame, you may find that this baby needs comfort and love. This is what we're trying to give it by taking drugs or overeating or trying to manipulate our relationships to bring us the comfort that we need on a deep primal level. But you can actually be with that infant in a state of healing. From your heart to his or her heart, you can bring comfort and love. You change the frequency or rate of vibration of these inner pictures, and you can create a state of healing to such a degree that many of the habits that you've been looking to for satisfaction and comfort can naturally fall away.

You can come into contact with the inner adolescent, bring reassurance and love. Past life selves can also be touched with the vibratory power. Many people have experienced abandonment in past lives when their tribes have left them. Others have starved to death and are therefore now hungry or in the habit of hoarding. Some have been gluttonous, and these behaviors have created results in the current lifetime. Many have been killed in battle, and they still carry the wounds, knives in their chests and nooses around their necks.

It's possible to lift up the vibration of all these experiences with love. Love is a sacred vibration, and it's a gift that is a tool for transformation. We can direct it like a laser beam to those places that are hanging out in the dark recesses of our souls, waiting to be reclaimed.

Great beings carry the love vibration.

The poet, Kabir wrote:

I hear bells ringing that no one has shaken,
inside "love" there is more joy than we know of,
rain pours down, although the sky is clear of clouds,
there are whole rivers of light.[1]

Kabir and other great ones have been sent to uplift us. Christ, Buddha, Moses, Mohammed, Mother Theresa, the Dalai Lama, Quan Yin, St. Germaine and more—all of these beings are paragons of love. They emanate the vibration of the heart and send the waves of love to heal us.

Ammachi, the great teacher, invites everyone to come up to greet her to receive radiations of healing love. Throngs of humanity flow up in streams to see this extraordinary beaming being of unconditional love. She hugs every single one—no ordinary hug, mind you, but a hug that brings you to the bosom of the divine mother. Smelling like an intoxicating garden of roses, she pulls people up to her and whispers mantras in their ears. She might actually wipe the faces of some people, wiping off their karmas, sweeping off lifetimes of grime. Sometimes she strokes the cheeks of others or touches their third eye to awaken the inner powers. These are ways in which she sends the love vibration. This helps people to shift their priorities, inspires them to meditate and encourages them to heal all the dark places inside. Great beings such as this are candles that ignite your own inner love.

Every great being is an inspiration. In remembering them, you can increase the rate of your own vibratory level and bring great love and healing to all parts of your self. Love brings the "All Oneness" that heals the aloneness of the soul.

Compassion is a deep awareness of the suffering of another, coupled with the wish to relieve it.

Compassion is an outgrowth of love, and it is a potent healing power. Henry Wadsworth Longfellow said, "If we could read the secret history of our enemies, we would find in each person's life, sorrow and suffering enough to disarm all hostility." In transformational healing, this doesn't mean that you are compassionate before you've allowed yourself to feel your outrage or your fear. You allow yourself to come to know whatever is inside of you. The process, as you remember, is "experience, release, and transform"—and we most often have to go through the full cycle in order to heal.

Everyone is suffering in one way or another. Some suffering is obvious; some is subtle. The fact is that few people in the world have found permanent happiness, and most suffer in their constant striving for approval, for pleasure, for respite from all kinds of hungers, for freedom from all kinds of thoughts and entanglements.

In healing, we look beneath the surface of our own or another's behavior. Looking deeply, we may see that the anger or restlessness or abruptness may be a hardened covering over another's pain and suffering. If one is willing, this is a perfect opportunity to go deeply within and assist him or her to experience the roots of the pain, to release and to heal.

Many of us wish to help alleviate our own and others' suffering. This compassion is not about "feeling sorry" for anyone. It's deeper than that. I had a friend named Sanje many years ago, and he was very wise. He had studied Tibetan Buddhism for a long time, and he had a radiant way of smiling that intimated that he knew something. One day I said to him, "Sanje, wouldn't it be wonderful if this were our last lifetime?" He looked at me with his beautiful smile and said, "Oh, I don't think that way. I'm just going to keep on coming back over and over to help until all beings are free from their suffering." This stunned and transformed me. From Sanje I learned about the dedication to service and compassion. His, I learned, was the Bodhisattva vow, the vow to serve until all beings are healed and free.

The way of service is the perfect path for many people. Some people, nevertheless, believe that everything is perfect as it is, that everything is an expression of both limitation and liberation, and that we need not do anything to attempt to change this perfect balance. Still, many of us are attuned to the way of service, and it is a natural expression as an outflow of the heart.

A compassionate healer will also foster compassion in another. There are so many ways in which this compassion can manifest:

- As compassion for the hurt parts of one's self. Instead of rejecting or abandoning these parts, telling them that they have to go away, you first have compassion for these parts. They were often originally rejected, and your telling them to leave only exacerbates the problem. This means that there may be compassion for the fragments of self—for the three year old or the teen or embryo or past life character or young adult of the current addict or unhappy overeater—all these parts can be healed with the power of compassion.

- As compassion for those who've wounded you, the perpetrators. This doesn't mean that forgiveness must come before you're ready. It does mean that eventually you come to see that everyone who makes another suffer is also suffering greatly and has also suffered at the hands of another.

There are profound ways of fostering compassion in healing.

Once I had a vision that I was standing on top of a mountain. Below in the valley, I saw my mother and father, and this time I saw them as individuals, not as parents. They were going around and around on the "wheel of life," having come here to earth to work out their own issues, suffering like everyone else. I could see them as human beings, and I was able to expand my ability to understand them.

To increase compassion, in your mind's eye, you can visit the childhood of parents or perpetrators. You can dive into another's psyche to understand their motivations. You can experience perpetrators' higher selves in order to heal the darkness. You can see all of it as a part of a divine plan for the ultimate enlightenment and edification of everyone. You don't need to obscure the emotions you feel—the anger, fear or resentment, but you can work toward a more expanded understanding and further open your capacities to heal. Sometimes by first experiencing indignation, rage, or sadness, you can move to the stages of "release and transform" in which you are able to experience the ultimate act of compassion—including the compassion you feel for yourself.

The compassion can expand even more, as you call in a naturally compassionate great being to magnify the healing. And then the healing expands even further as the understanding of a compassionate universe takes hold. This is the understanding that, from a certain vantage point, all things that happen are for the highest good, that there is a positive force guiding the flow of events, that even as the universe gives us difficult lessons and experiences, there is compassion behind them. We are being awakened through all the experiences of our lives, awakened to the knowledge of the love that lies at the core of existence.

A woman named Sandra was very sensitive. She was always having her feelings hurt, and she experienced perpetrators all around her. She went within herself and found a little girl who was afraid of the other children. They always hurt her feelings. Her parents also hurt her feelings. Everyone did. So she, the adult, held the little girl close to her, stroked her head and comforted her, told her of her worth, her beauty and her strength, told her how much she was loved. She then became twelve and twenty and forty, and all of these past selves became equally loved. Then a figure of infinite mercy and compassion, the Quan Yin, came to her and touched her with the touch of the most profound love and said to her, "It doesn't matter who hurts your feelings. These are just problems of your ego self. No matter at all. Understand how everyone is suffering. Understand how everyone is seeking some way out—through recognition or superiority, through some way or another. Remember, my dear one, that you are looking for your feelings to be hurt so that you can heal a fundamental error in understanding. You are looking for the repetition of this feeling inside so that you can ultimately drop this game of the ego and come to Me. I love you infinitely, and I ask you now to remain in peace and equanimity and love. I am your guidance and your love." She then touched with love the five year old, the twelve and twenty and forty year old, and brought them all into truth. Sandra could then love the ones she felt were persecuting her, as their pain was great. She even stroked their heads in infinite compassion and told them what she had been told. In this way, she achieved balance, and in this way, she was healed.

The ability to shift perception is a
gift of higher consciousness.

Next to love and compassion, our ability to view life from an expanded perspective is a profound gift. Witness consciousness, the capacity to stand back and see the panorama of events of our lives on the screen of awareness, is a high healing state. Some healing modalities use visualizations that entail sitting in a movie theater and watching yourself on screen, making changes in the movie, ultimately making changes in your life.

Witness consciousness is a state of meditation. You are watching yourself as an actor in the play. You are not even the director. You are the observer, and from this point of view, healing takes place. When you expand awareness this way, you are in touch with a high level of truth. In its highest level of truth, the real you is the one who is able to witness, to observe without judgment. From this vantage point, clarity comes, and it may reveal truths such as:

- Whatever has taken place has contributed to the growth of your soul, and it is therefore necessary.

- Everyone is working out something or other in his or her own life plan, and if you can extricate yourself from it for a moment, you can see it more clearly.

- Issues of self-esteem, hurt, fear, victimization and more are issues of a limited understanding.

- All experiences of our lives are opportunities for enlightenment and grace, all pointing to our ultimate upliftment in consciousness.

- If we truly saw underneath all of it, we could do nothing but forgive.

Sarah was abused by her father, and he later molested her daughters. She needed first to experience her profound outrage and to let it come to her awareness. After a time, she was able to float above her life. She saw that her father was sick, and she saw that in some way everyone had learned something from their experiences. Everyone had been deepened; everyone had needed to look within and begin the path of healing. She experienced some divine voices that said to her, "Your difficulties have been given to you so you can help others to forgive." Helping others in this way shifted the focus of her life.

A woman named Ellen had terrible abuse in her childhood. At age four, she was burned by a blowtorch on much of her body. The family told her that it was an accident, but she had an instinctual knowing that it happened because of her father's rage. The adult part of her healed and comforted this beautiful little girl and her burn wounds. She saw the burned child healed in the light, and she experienced the child as an angel. She used to feel victimized, but now she shifted her whole view of life. In the cosmic view she saw that all her experiences had contributed to the growth of her soul. Through this, she came alive, and a new spiritual quality entered her life. Up until this point, she'd been hiding, afraid to interact with people, tucked away inside herself. Now she is animated and alive, as she sees the larger perspective for her life.

A man named Joseph thought he was ugly. As he relaxed, he experienced a darkness in his heart center. As he paid attention to it and watched it from within, the darkness began to move, to split open, and a light exploded from within him. He then felt the love for himself pouring through him, and he realized his own beauty as a fountain that comes from inside.

Seeing the cosmic overview doesn't mean that we don't need to stand up to perpetrators or to take abuse. It does mean that here is an additional road to empowerment, an inner solution that sees the greater dimensions of experience. There is so much more in heaven and earth than we have dreamed of, and we are invited to expand our ability to see it. In parts 5 and 6, you'll find many more techniques for experiencing this. The development of a healing consciousness is one of the greatest gifts of our existence.

If you look at the darkness, you can find the light.

Embrace it, all that seems dark.
Embrace it, all that seems unlovable.
Embrace it, and be whole again…
O traveler, let nothing go by.
Let nothing be denied.
Let the child inside cry.
Darkness is known by the light.
…How about loving the fearful
Into wholeness, holy Oneness.
…Embrace it, and be whole again.

Kathy Zavada [2]

In our culture, we are taught two opposite ends of a continuum of behavior. One is to run from darkness, to tranquilize or anesthetize ourselves against it. Another is to take it in incessantly in the media and many other ways.

There is, however, a third way, and that is to pay attention to the darkness and thereby transmute it. This is the essence of transformational healing. What this means is that we can go to the "underworld" within us to learn power, strength and fire as empowering qualities that enhance the good. If we deny the dark forces, push them down, they reappear as jack-in-the-boxes, popping up in other places, at other times.

A woman named Susan started her life in a very dark way. She was born in Japan to a beautiful but troubled Japanese mother and an equally troubled English father. When her father took his own life because he'd been caught in an infidelity, her mother couldn't or wouldn't take care of her, so she was put up for adoption. She had a few very hard years until an American missionary family finally adopted her. They were very kind, but she didn't feel connected with them, and she was left with deep emotions of fear, anger and abandonment. "I don't deserve to be loved," she'd say. "They gave me away." This theme wove itself throughout her life, at work and in all of her relationships. She wanted to feel connected, but it was very difficult.

One day, in a state of deep relaxation, she felt a tightness and a fear in her upper chest. Instead of immediately getting rid of it, she decided to look at it. She was standing at the mouth of a dark cave, like a black hole in space. The feelings of fear, anger, sadness, and pain began to swirl up in the air, and she began to swirl with them inside her mind. She went very far back into her being, back to before her own birth, in which she realized that she'd contracted for a very challenging assignment in her life so that she could learn humility. Still in that swirling energy of fear, anger, sadness and pain, she felt a great transformation happening. It was becoming passion instead. She realized that the cave was the womb, and she was the baby. The fear was coming from the baby's mother. She reached down into the entrance of the cave and brought the baby out—only this time, her dear grandmother, her Obachan, was there, drawing the baby up into the light. The three of them were now surrounded by light, and spirit was helping them to heal the old anger and fear.

We have said many times that "the way out is through." The more we are willing to penetrate and transmute the darkness, the more we are able to shine the light with greater intensity and brilliance.

We are living embodiments of spiritual essence, and light is at our source. We came here to work with light, to turn up its intensity, to remember it. In that is our connection with the infinite. In the Tarot, the Hermit walks in a dark area—but he is carrying a lantern. And so, of course, are we.

In Star Wars, Obi Wan Kenobi says to Darth Vader, "If you strike me down, I shall become more powerful than you could ever imagine." The brighter we shine our light, the greater contribution we make to the transmutation of the dark forces and the transformation of the world.

Part Four

The Energy System

There is a miraculous way of tapping the healing power by working with the meridian system.

One way to work with our issues is to bring pure awareness and inner healing to them. Another is to work directly with the energy system. This shifts our electromagnetic energies, returning us to a state of peace and healing. When Mark Douglas introduced me to the "tapping techniques," I became aware that I was being given one of the great secrets of the universe.

The technique involves tapping on various points on the body while using specific verbalizations to eliminate or reduce all kinds of pain and suffering. It's amazingly simple and easy to learn, and yet its results are phenomenal. As I became more and more involved with using the techniques with clients and with myself, I found variations that embellished their power. In part 7, you'll find specific directions for using these techniques. We often combine these techniques with deep inner healing. They can also be used on their own or in combination with many other modalities.

An eleven-year-old boy named Jonah had been bitten by a pit bull the year before when he was ten. He had developed enormous phobias, and he'd been in therapy and on medication. He was a sweet boy; yet I could feel the fear in his closed body language and shallow breathing. The medication wasn't working; nor were other techniques his mother had him try. His mother brought him to see me, and I told him I'd like to do some tapping on special points while saying specific words about his problem. He had developed many fears after his traumatic experience with the pit bull. In the first round of tapping, his fear of rain left him completely. Next the fear of thunder and lightning was gone. His mother said to him, "Are you sure you don't feel that fear anymore? You don't have to say you're fine just to please us." The boy said, "Oh yes, I feel happy. I don't feel that fear anymore." Then he eliminated his morbid fear of all kinds of dogs. Next, he released his awful fear of bugs. He felt uplifted and joyful. His mother was amazed. One week later, he went on a trip to Disneyland without his previous medications. He did splendidly—free from his fears and very relaxed.

Not long after that, I went to a fair. I was walking down a road when a woman came up to me, and with anguish on her face, she said, "Do you have any aspirin or ibuprofen? My daughter has such bad cramps that she can't walk. They just came on suddenly." I smiled to myself that she was guided in my direction, and I told her that I didn't have any aspirin or ibuprofen, but I had something else that we could use: I could tap her with my fingers. She was ready to try anything, so I began to tap her thirteen-year-old daughter. Within one round of tapping (less than thirty seconds), the cramps had almost disappeared. Within the next thirty seconds, the cramps were gone completely. Her parents' faces showed total astonishment. I was thrilled to have a first-aid kit in my fingertips.

The technique works with the human energy system, which circulates through our bodymind in channels or meridians. You tap on specific points to stimulate the free flow of energy through the meridians. As you tap on a point, neuro-receptors under the skin convert the pressure to an electrical impulse that is transmitted to the brain. This is combined with the power of mind or intention. As you focus on a specific problem, you send out your intention for healing it. At the same time, you create a physiological response by tapping on the points. This process has its roots in ancient Chinese medical understanding of meridians and energy systems: in acupressure, in acupuncture, in meditation, in prayer, in the great healing modalities of the world.

In the same way that a computer responds by having a human being tap on its keys, or a television responds to remote control, so too can signals be given to the energy system of the human organism.

*Energy is the substrata of all existence,
and we can help it to flow more freely.*

The entire universe is made of energy. It is the basis of all that is. This energy exists as the substrata of all existence. It is electromagnetic and intelligent, and we can experience how it is organized into systems by looking at all the forms around us—especially human systems. Tapping on gateways to the channels in which energy flows is a key to allowing energy to flow more freely, to create healing and open the gateways of human consciousness.

Everything can benefit from an increased flow of healing energy and from the intention of the mind to heal. Here are some of the human issues that have been positively influenced by working with energy: addictive cravings (food, cigarettes, alcohol, drugs), allergies, anxiety and panic attacks, anger, compulsions, depression and sadness, dyslexia, self image and self esteem. Other issues are: grief and loss, guilt, insomnia, negative memories, nightmares, pain, physical symptoms (fibromyalgia, arthritis, back & neck pain) and other physical healing. Other situations helped with tapping are: peak performance (golf, public speaking, performing in public), post traumatic stress disorder, sexual abuse issues, all kinds of fears and phobias (bridges, being alone, claustrophobia, computers, dentists, flying, driving, elevators, heights, needles, public speaking, fear of snakes or spiders) and many more.

A woman named Ann who, when marrying her husband for the second time, still retained deep old fears that once again the marriage would fall apart. Even though he said he'd changed and grown, his wife could not fully be present in the relationship now because she was so paralyzed with fear. She had enough faith to take the vows again, but her grief and old self esteem issues were very much in the way. Within moments of tapping, she stopped crying and knew that she could open up to him once again. She discovered that underneath all of this

was the voice of her mother telling her that she wasn't
pretty or smart enough (Cinderella, truly.) She tapped
that away as well and went home with a smile. She
subsequently became more open and self confident and is
now more connected with her spiritual source of strength
and faith. She is also doing well in her marriage.

There are a number of variations to this technique, as
you will see in part 7. You can do it on yourself or on
another. If you are a practitioner, feel free to use it with
your clients or patients. Feel free to combine it with other
modalities. If this is your first experience with a healing
technique you will find it simple, and you may well be
amazed at the results. Combined with transformational
healing or just by itself, it is a major healing discovery.

You are working with bioelectricity and language for healing.

You could speculate at length as to how and why this
special tapping technique works. You can rest assured it's
about "energy." Energy is the life force of the universe. It's
the electromagnetic field that underlies all that is, the
vitality in all creation. We are working with this energy
field when we use this technique.

The human energy field is similar to other kinds of
electrical systems. When there is a disruption in a
mechanism, you notice static or noise. In the case of
humans, you notice various kinds of impediments or

problems. When you are able to dissolve the static or noise, you can help the mechanism to run smoothly, with fewer disruptions. Your TV or computer, for example, runs more smoothly by making some adjustments. So, too, does the human energy system. Almost as if you had a remote control or a keyboard, you can "tap in" the appropriate code, which will create more peace in the system, help the energy to smooth out and work optimally.

There may also be a biological component to the success with tapping techniques. By tapping on acupressure points, you are stimulating and releasing endorphins, the pleasure chemicals that send well being signals to your brain.

There is the additional component of language in the tapping process. You don't simply tap; you talk, as well. You talk about the original dilemmas, and your phrasing focuses the healing process. You talk about the problems using negative phrases, not positive ones.

Now this is very interesting, as you would think that tapping alone could put the bioelectrical system back into alignment. But there is another component. When we verbally state the problems, we are speaking to the consciousness in the specific areas or issues of our bodymind. Combined with tapping, there is a powerful healing response created by the synergy of both the words and the tapping.

Many metaphysicians and yogis have spoken about consciousness in the organ systems and in the entire human system. They have talked about how this consciousness responds to a mind/body approach to healing.

Yogi Ramacharacka, in his book, *The Science of Psychic Healing,*[3] has said: "...the organs, parts, and even cells of the body have 'mind' in them.... This 'mind' in the cells, cell-groups, nerve centres, ganglia, etc., responds to a strong thought impression from outside..." What the yogi is saying is that there are communities of cells in each organ system that have their own collective consciousness. So the liver may have its own consciousness, as may the heart and lungs. One may feel sluggish and need to "awaken." Another may feel congested or may be carrying stresses and hurts from onslaughts of the past.

This is very significant, as there is a potent mind/body connection at work in the human organism. Still even more significant is that these systems respond powerfully to "thought impressions" and prompting from both within and without.

Many healers have seen over and over the power of verbal suggestions on the cells of the physical body and on the emotions. In addition, the practice of mindfulness, in which we pay attention to whatever is at hand, brings a powerful awareness to the issue and creates significant change through that attention.

We combine this verbal attention with a natural physiological response, which comes from tapping on energy points. What we get is a combination of electricity, biology and consciousness. The smoothing out of the electrical pathways, combined with the biochemical production of endorphins and other biochemical elements, combined with our connection with consciousness—all create a powerful healing response. We're working here with specific acupuncture points and the ancient healing pathways called meridians. We are also contacting the consciousness of the bodymind with our words and with our intention.

You might even say that each time we state the issue, it is like a tiny "prayer" sent in the direction of the distress. And the tap is like a knock on the door of the bodymind. Whatever may be the explanation for how it works, it works.

Combining energy therapy with transformational healing creates extraordinary healing.

You can use the tapping techniques before you do deep relaxation to clear yourself or a client, and you can also do the tapping as a release technique during the deep relaxation healing process.

A young woman named Tina had a tendency, actually an intense *samskara*, for worrying. She would look at the worst possible scenario from just about any life situation that would present itself to her. Just beginning graduate school, she worried about failing or not getting good grades. Then she worried about not finding a job, as no one would employ her. She worried that her relationship would break up, and she'd have to live penniless—and it would be the end of the world, as well. She worked herself up into states that she called paranoia. So we did some energy therapy with her before beginning our deep relaxation. We tapped on energy points verbalizing such issues as: worrying about life; fearing the worst; making herself unhappy. We moved her fears from a very high level of intensity to a very low level.

Then we began to do some deep relaxation. She saw herself in a gray-blue fog. There was a tunnel there, and it led into an abyss. She fell into it, and it was cold. She was alone and didn't want to be there. She felt lost, and her hair and clothing were all disheveled. She was walking around in the fog.

As she relaxed, we did some more energy therapy, as we said the words "walking along in a fog" and "feeling lost." She noticed that she needed some shoes. And it occurred to her that someone might help her get them. She began to feel a gigantic hand stretching out to her. Something was now buoying her up. She said, "This is the hand of God." She saw another room there—like a hut. She went in and felt very comfortable. Her clothes were less disheveled, and she had on some shoes. It seemed to her that the hand of God went into that room too.

She had brought this alienated fragment of herself into wholeness. She gave it grounding (shoes). She gave it protection (a new room to go into, sheltered by the "hand of God"). She was no longer in a fog. She was now able to integrate this wholeness into her being, and she began to see a new scenario for her life.

The very act of paying attention to her distress, combined with tapping, had led her to the resolution of the very mind patterns that were creating her dilemma. She entered a dimension of awareness that was transcendental.

She came to realize that even if the worst scenario did take place, she had all the resources within herself to handle whatever comes. Most of all, she understood that we don't really know what is "good or bad," as there are jewels at the core of every life experience. She now knows she can become the witness of her thinking process in the future. She knows that she can tell herself to choose her thought processes. She also can tap herself whenever the worries come up, and she can continue to create wholeness. She can keep the spiral of her consciousness moving in an upward direction.

It is possible to combine energy therapy with many different modalities. It's simple, and it works.

Part Five

Healing Processes for You to Do

1.

Healing the
Mind and Consciousness

Working with Samskaras or Thought Patterns

- Become aware of a repetitive pattern of your mind. Look at what function it plays in your life, what it is doing for you. Look at what might have been its origin. Find out when the pattern is most predominant in your life. See how you might be experiencing it in your body.

- Tap on yourself to release the hold of the pattern. (See part 7, p. 214.)

- Contact your higher self for healing and transformation of the pattern. Relax, and ask your higher being to speak to you in words of wisdom, to remind you of your true nature. In your inner mind, let your higher being remind you of the ultimate truth. You may hear such reminders of the truth from within as, "I AM the power of healing," or, "You are a divine being of light."

- Ask for a sign or symbol to remind yourself of these greater truths, (such as putting your thumb together with your index finger). You may also receive some visual form of empowerment, or you may experience yourself beaming with light.

- Remind yourself that you are not a victim of your thought patterns, that you have the tools for transforming them. "I am the healing power of the universe, and I am healing myself now."

❋ Stilling the Mind Meditation

- Sit or lie down in a comfortable place. Close your eyes, and pay attention to your breathing.

- Coordinate a mantra with your breathing.

- You can use: *MA OM*

  (*Ma* is universal love; *om* is universal consciousness.)

  > or *HAM SA* (I am that)

  > or OM *NAMAH SHIVAYA* (I honor my Self)

  > or *I AM*

  The first syllable is repeated on the inhalation; the second, on the exhalation.

- Say the mantra silently to yourself. Go deeply within. Keep your concentration on the gentle breathing and on your mantra. If thoughts come in, that's fine. Just bring yourself back to the awareness of your breathing and on the mantra as soon as you're able.

- Do this on a regular basis, at a designated time, for as long a period as you like. As you maintain a discipline, you find rewards of greater peace and ease in your daily life.

Experiencing, Releasing and Transforming: Exploring the Darkness on the Way to the Light

- Pay attention to an issue or a feeling or a physical manifestation that has been bothering you.

- Relax enough to explore it as fully as possible. If it had words, what might it say?

- If this were a part of you, who would it be? Would it be the form of a person? A symbol? A mythical character or quality?

- Find an earlier experience that directly relates to this. See what the earlier influences might be. Go back as far as your inner mind wishes to take you.

- See what role this issue is playing in your life? Has it been impeding your progress? Keeping you safe? Making you stronger?

- Explore what feelings you may have about it.

- Create a statement of the problem, giving it a name, such as "my fear of success" or "my grief about loss" or "my inability to move on."

- Do some tapping on the problem—using either the Emotional Freedom Techniques (p. 214) or the "Root Cause Technique" (p. 234).

- Do some of the transformational healing techniques, as they appear in part 6 (p. 143). What might be an appropriate healing influence for you? Would you like to bring in healing guidance or wisdom? Would you like to see the advantage in the situation? Would you like to bring in a compassionate healing figure or force? See what other healing influences might be good for you.

- Make a special healing tape for yourself, as explained in part 6 (p. 193).

- Give yourself a great deal of love.

Understanding the Wounded Healer Paradigm

- Explore how your early life (and past lives, if appropriate) have contributed to your healing abilities. See how any difficulties you've endured have created healing power in you.

- Find any literature that discusses the trials of shamans and healers, and see how going to the "underworld" is often a necessary step in becoming a transcendent force for healing. (See John Sanford's *Healing and Wholeness*[4] for a good discussion of this paradigm of the wounded healer.)

2.

Healing Emotions

Resolving Difficult Feelings or Patterns

- Pay close attention to a deep feeling inside yourself. Perhaps it is fear, anger, grief, shame or guilt. Experience whatever emotion is present, and explore it as fully as possible. Can you experience it in your body, and if so, where? Can you describe any and all manifestations of this feeling? If it had a color, what might that be? If it had a shape, what shape might it be? If it were a person, and if it could speak, what might it say? Greet this feeling, and explore the roots of this feeling as deeply as possible.

- Watch the feeling go through shifts as you become aware of it.

- You may want to describe it to someone else as you explore it. Or you may want to write about it, watching it move and change as you progress.

- When you're ready to release, you can do any or all of the following release techniques:

  - Hold an actual balloon in your hands. When you're ready to release your fear, anger or deep experience, talk to the balloon as if it were a perpetrator of your issue. You may be speaking to a parent who abused you or a mate who you feel abandoned you or to a teacher who didn't hear you. Press your thumbs into the balloon as hard as you can, and let it burst when you're ready. Use as many balloons as you feel you need to. With the loud noise of the balloon, a release happens in the entire nervous system. There is usually a complete calm afterwards. At this point, you're ready for the transformation into peace, understanding and love.

- Simply watch whatever is taking place in your body and mind. Allow shifts to take place naturally in your feelings and thoughts through the activity of pure awareness.

- Tap on the emotional experience, and resolve it by working with the energy system. Use either the tapping technique (p. 214) or the Root Cause Technique (p. 234)—or both of them.

- Comfort those parts of self that need comfort by holding a pillow, and give love to that part of yourself that needs solace.

- Imagine the part of you that is hurting on one side of your inner mind. Notice everything you can—your age, your feeling, your appearance. Then imagine another you—one that is healed and whole, radiant, alive and compassionate. Bring the two selves together, so the healed one brings love and comfort to the hurting one. Let the healed one bring in healing wisdom. (Some examples of this are: "This wasn't the right relationship for you. You're ready for a new life." Or "Your dear ones had to go to the other side at this time, but you can feel their love if you open your heart to their presence.") Then allow the two parts, the hurting and the healed, to merge in this love. Experience a sense of great wholeness. You are bringing old fragments of yourself into the whole, creating a new unity in your being.

- Say farewell to an old habit of mind or feeling or person by sending it or him or her off in a balloon in your inner mind.

- Play a chime, and send away the difficult experience, releasing it with the sound of the chime, visualizing its release in any way that might be appropriate for you.

- Bring in any of the resources of higher consciousness that are meaningful for you. Open your heart to healing love. You can open the channels for a great being to bring in healing. You can allow healing wisdom to come forth, and you can explore what contribution this experience might be making to your life, as you reframe it or see it in an expanded way. You can experience light, perhaps as beams coming from or to your heart from the universe, shifting your consciousness into a state of healed oneness. You can imagine this light emanating from within yourself, like a sun beaming from your heart, your solar plexus, and your "third eye center." Feel it sending rays of healing throughout your entire being, then out to the others in your immediate environment, and ultimately out farther to include the rest of humanity and the entire universe.

- Explore the life lessons in all of your experiences, and see what your soul has needed to understand. See the panoramic view of your life, and let the soul lessons reveal themselves to you.

✣ Deeply Exploring Root Causes

- Find an issue in your life that you would like to understand more fully. Relax deeply or use muscle testing to discover the root causes. (See part 6, p. 234.)

- See how the problem originates from the original "illusion of separation."

- Then look at the rest of these issues, and discover which may apply to you and in what particular ways:

  - Does this have to do with a *samskara*, a tendency of the mind that you've brought in since birth?

  - Is it about something that happened in your childhood? With parents? Siblings? Anyone else?

  - Could it be about a wound that you've picked up that belonged to someone else—parents, teachers, or others?

  - Might it be something that took place while you were in the womb? Or an experience at your birth?

  - Is it something that might have been from a past life?

- Could this be a subpersonality or part of you who needs attention and healing?

- What does this have to do with a core belief of yours? And how is this forming a comfort zone for you?

- Have you had a previous trauma?

- Is this a metaphor for something taking place in your consciousness?

- Is it a way of getting a basic and primal need met?

- Is this a recurring pattern that is asking for healing?

- How might it best be healed?

- What is it here to teach you?

- How can you transform your consciousness into higher understanding?

- Relax and put your awareness on a traumatic experience. If this is difficult, stand back and explore as if it were a play. (This is witness consciousness, a state of pure observation.) You can write about this or simply allow yourself to experience it in your inner mind. It may be necessary to have another person with you to help create a feeling of protection and to "hold the space for you," or you can do it on your own. In exploring the situation, see what emotions you're experiencing. Look to see what images are present, as well as who is there. With courage, allow yourself to know what is happening in your inner mind—in as much or as little detail as you feel prepared to experience. You may want to put light around the experience to give it a healing context.

- Tap on the traumatic experience, using either the tapping technique (p. 214) or any of the variations, especially the Root Cause Technique (p. 234). Find the appropriate phrase to tap on. You may want to start with the emotion that you're feeling. Then you can go into other aspects of the original trauma. This will help you to handle the deep emotional experiences that arise.

- Take care of the part of yourself that has been traumatized. Heal and soothe the wounds. You can hold that fragment of yourself, by holding a pillow and bringing in soothing love. You can bring in a great being or a guide. You can beam soothing healing light. You can even allow that wounded part of self to become strong and stand up to the situation. You can make changes in the old inner "photograph" of the event by shifting the details of the original event, and you can help that part of yourself that has been in a state of shock to awaken into a new state of light and healing.

- If you like, you can work with the perpetrator. Find out what has been going on in his or her life to create such a person. You can reduce his or her power. You can tap on any or all feelings about the perpetrator. You can use an actual balloon, blow it up, tie it, and talk to it as if it were the perpetrator. As you talk to the perpetrator, you become more and more powerful, and by the time you actually break the balloon, you feel exceedingly strong. Breaking the balloon releases the energy, pulls it out of the nervous system and defuses much or all of the traumatic material. Energy therapy works very well for this also.

- You can work more subtly—change the colors in the inner picture from bright to muted, change the sounds from loud to soft, move the perpetrator or the incident farther away. (NLP, or neurolinguistic programming, calls these inner experiences "submodalities.") You can put up a wall, close the door, and somehow make the perpetrator less threatening.

- You may wish to "cut the cords" that bind you to the perpetrator. These are usually found at the solar plexus, heart center or third eye. You can imagine the cord or cords and then imagine pulling them out. (See Transformational Healing Techniques, p. 143.)

- You can send the incident to a "trash can" or "recycle bin" in your internal mind or biocomputer. You can float up above the situation of the trauma, shift around any aspects of it that you like. Instead of being in hell, you can blow out the fires. You can put a light of healing around the entire traumatic experience.

- You can also stand back and view it with the wisdom of your soul.

- Your own inner wisdom will tell you how you might want to view this event with expanded understanding. It might lead you, for example to see the karmic overview of the situation. This might mean, for example, that you understand that you and the perpetrator may have needed to resolve something or that the incident was a catalyst for your awakening.

- You may be ready for the ultimate healing act of forgiveness. This lifts up the situation and brings grace to your soul. This is where you see that each player in the drama was doing the best he or she could according to his or her level of consciousness at the moment. You can forgive yourself. In this action is great freedom. The Root Cause Technique (p. 234) can assist you with this.

- You can understand that the situation was a part of the drama of your life—not the essence. You can fully experience how it is no longer happening, and in fact it belongs actually to the realm of illusion. You can remember that now you've awakened from that dream, and you can come into presence in this very moment.

Healing Fragments of Self
or Subpersonalities

- Find and experience a fragment or part of yourself that has been in an unloved state within you. See it as a personality. Explore that part of yourself. See what he or she is feeling or doing. See the state of her physical body. What is the position of her body? Is her head up or down? Is she huddled in a corner or standing up?

- Ask her what she needs. Usually she needs love, and this is your opportunity to bring love to her. This may come from you, and you may want to hold an actual pillow as you bring love to this part. You can bring love from another source, such as a great being, a grandparent, a guide or from the divine Source in the form of light or in whatever way you might receive divine love.

- You may also want to change the environment and circumstances she has been in for so long. You can activate the "frozen picture" of this part of yourself and bring this part to life. You may want to imagine this part as whole and healed. Ultimately she can become united and aligned with you and your highest nature.

Transforming Internal Saboteurs

- If you're looking at changing a habit or shifting some aspect of yourself, complete the following sentence:

  "I don't want to _____ (whatever the contemplated change may be) because _____." Don't think hard about the answer; just say what's on the top of your head.

- When you complete the sentence, see if you need to go further with this: "And I don't want to _____ because _____." Keep going until you find exactly what's in the way of doing or being or having what a part of yourself would like. (Full details and examples of this technique called ReSourcing, p. 147.)

- When you find out what's in the way (the saboteurs), you find a part of yourself that has specific needs. These needs may be to feel more comfortable and safe or to not "rock the boat" of your life. See how you can fulfill these needs in ways other than self-sabotaging ones.

3.

Healing the Energy System

Tapping Away Your Difficulties

- Get in touch with something that has been bothering you. It may be a physical or emotional pain. It may be some craving or habit. It may be an old trauma that has not been resolved.

- Find a way to verbally express this situation, such as "this pain in my back." If this is a situation that is not current, see how well you can imagine it.

- Rate the intensity of the situation from zero to ten, ten being the most intense.

- Begin the tapping process, as described on p. 214. Remember to do the "setup" by saying, "Even though I have this back pain (or whatever your problem might be), I deeply, completely accept myself." Then proceed to tap on the points, saying "back pain" each time.

- When you complete one round of tapping, assess the intensity again.

- Do another round if needed, this time saying "remaining back pain"—or your own situation. Assess the intensity again, and continue until you get the intensity numbers as low as possible.

4.

Healing with Higher Consciousness

Calling to the Higher Self

- To get in touch with a transcendent experience of your higher being, you can engage in the practice of calling to it. You might have some key words that invoke this presence. Some of them might be:

  - *"I AM"*

    These words are geared to bring forth an experience of the higher being. As you say them, you may want to include the power of your intention to reach higher awareness. These words might precede an affirmative statement, such as "I AM the power of healing." Or "I AM connected with all that is." You may want to visualize a beam of light coming into the top of your head as you say these words. You may then want to follow that light all the way down into your third eye, your heart center, and then the rest of your body, bringing illumination to your being.

  - *"I give thanks…"*

    These words can invoke the "attitude of gratitude" that will shift your consciousness and bring a higher awareness to your life. Any time you use them, you can feel bathed in a more expanded presence.

- *Any name for the higher presence that uplifts you.*

  The word "God" or "Goddess" ignites the consciousness of some. Or you may be connected with a form of higher consciousness, such as Jesus, Buddha, Krishna, Quan Yin, Moses, Saint Germaine—or any other manifestation that opens you to the illumined life.

- *Pure Awareness*

  You can still your mind by paying close attention to the moment. This will quite naturally open the doors for higher consciousness. The stillness of your thoughts will open up spaces in your awareness for pure being to manifest. It may help you to focus on the life energy that flows within your body. This will keep you centered and focused on pure being.

Opening the Channels of Love

- *Explore what might be in the way of love:*

  - Look at the child within and see if this one has been held back in a frozen past self. See how you might "unfreeze" this picture, bring it to life, and bring love and healing to this child.

  - Explore incidents of past hurts leading to bitterness and lack of love. See them as opportunities to advance on the path of spirit rather than as detriments. Bring love to your past selves that have been hurt, and open them to receive a touch of love—both human and divine.

  - Explore how it feels in your heart center. Is it open or closed? Is there a wall, a feeling of tension or an open space? If you find a closed space, ask your bodymind what it might need in order to open more fully. Listen to it, and as you do, it will tell you what the next step might be.

- *Tap into the ocean of love.*

  - Remember someone or something that invokes the feeling of love in you. This can be a loving grandmother, a trusted friend, an affectionate parent or child—or the very loving part of your own self. Let this love spread throughout your being. Find a word or phrase that symbolizes this love, and say it over and over with your thumb held together with your index finger as a signal. Remind yourself that you can say this word any time, and you'll come back to this experience of love.

- Imagine a light emanating from your heart center, and let it open you more and more.

- Bring into your awareness, a great being, such as Christ, Buddha, Mother Theresa or any great teacher with whom you have an affinity. Experience this one as a generator of extraordinary love.

- Get in touch with an angelic force or inner guide who lifts you up into that supreme level of love.

- Bring love to the unloved parts of yourself. Find this love at your essence. Make contact with the parts of yourself that feel alienated and alone. You may want to hold or hug them, stroke them, take them away from harmful environments, give them words of encouragement, become their parent or friend. To give this love, you might want to experience a radiant version of yourself. You might be beaming with light, strong, confident and wise. You may want to embrace these other parts of yourself (the ones that we all usually reject), transforming and integrating them into your essential being.

- You can experience a more abstract form of universal love. You may feel this energy emanating from the universe and penetrating your heart center, filling up your entire being. It may also emanate from inside of you, as you are the universe in microcosm. This way you can shift the vibratory level of your body and mind, lifting up your experiences and healing your life.

- Experience the expanded state of gratitude, a consciousness level of great love and healing power. You can be grateful for all you've undergone, all those who haven't met your needs, all the rejection and hurt you've experienced—because all of those experiences have turned you toward higher consciousness and contributed to your evolution on the path of the heart.

Expanding Capacities for Compassion

- Look at an incident or a person in a compassionate way. Recall, for example, someone or something that has been difficult. In your mind's eye, stand on top of a mountain, and see what life lessons or difficult circumstances that person may be working through. See what the childhood of that difficult person might have been like. Or see how your own difficult situation might be leading you forward on the path of the spirit. See with expanded perspective.

- Imagine a truly compassionate being. This can be one you know or a great teacher or healer—or it might even be yourself. Experience how this one might view your life experience. Let yourself experience the quality of that compassion and how it can uplift your life.

- Feel the compassion of the universe by looking at the advantages of the difficulties in our own life and in the larger world picture. For example, look at how losing a home might have been the opportunity to release the past and begin a new life. Or see how having been abused has led you to the path of the spirit, opened you to compassion and made you strong.

Seeing from the Expanded Perspective

- Look at an event or experience in your life that has been particularly difficult. Stand back from it enough to see what contributions it has made to the growth of your soul.

  - What strengths have you gained from it?

  - How has it helped you to burn off your karmas?

  - How has this contributed to your evolution as a wounded healer?

  - How has it led you to your spiritual path?

  - What has it been attempting to teach you?

  - What aspects of your character have transformed because of this experience?

  - How has it opened you to wisdom and compassion for the suffering of all beings?

  - What blessings are contained in the difficulties?

- In your mind's eye, imagine that you're standing on a mountaintop or floating above the scenarios of your life or seeing these experiences on a screen. As you look down or onto the screen, you can see people and events from your life in more expanded ways.

  - Observe the childhood of someone in your life. See what life situations have created the kind of person he or she has become.

- See people from your life as beings working out their issues on the wheel of life. See them from an evolutionary perspective, growing and changing with the life lessons they're receiving.

- Call upon any transcendent forces to assist you in seeing your situations from the larger perspective. Invite in your I AM consciousness or highest wisdom or great beings such as Buddha, Christ, Quan Yin, or Moses. Call to guides or angels to uplift your vision and bring forth cosmic understanding.

- Find a word or a phrase, an image or an inner gift that can serve as a reminder of your expanded view.

- Experience the divine energy inherent in all things. Allow yourself to come to know a dimension of consciousness that sees everything as energy. Here the distinctions and sorrows transform into a more ecstatic level of being.

Inviting In the Great Beings

- Understand that one of the great gifts given to us is the presence of extraordinary masters of love and enlightenment. Call upon them to uplift your own vision as well as the suffering of humanity.

- Either find a great being with whom you feel a great affinity, or choose one of those below. Imagine the presence and allow healing of all of your sorrows and difficulties. Imagine that wisdom is issuing forth from this great one, and listen to what this wisdom offers you.

- Explore this list—or find one of your own:

  - Lord Gautama, the Buddha—great world wisdom teacher who taught the path of pure mind, detachment and right living.

  - Quan Yin—great goddess and Mother of Mercy and Compassion, loved and revered throughout the world. Female aspect of the Buddha and an expression of the divine mother.

  - Jesus Christ—great avatar and light for humanity, healer and transcender of death, embodiment of infinite love and the Christ Consciousness.

  - Krishna—Hindu aspect of God who enchanted all with his extraordinary magnetism.

- St. Germaine—one of the "ascended masters" who took his body into light and still works in the "lighter realms."

- Others: Mother Mary, Shiva, Sri Yukteswar, Paramahansa Yogananda, Mata Amritanandamayi, Sri Ramakrishna, Sai Baba, Ananda Mayi Ma, Nityananda, Archangel Michael or Gabriel, Meher Baba, Babaji, Papaji, Maitreya, Mother Theresa, Moses, the Karmapa, the Dalai Lama—and you can add your own.

Welcoming Inner Guidance and Wisdom

- After you've come through the "experience, release and transform" process, ask your Wise Mind to be with you. Ask it to tell you or show you anything else you might want to know about the situation at hand. Ask it to give you perspective. Ask it what the situation has been trying to tell you or what meaning it might have for your life. Ask it what might be your next step. Ask it if there is any stone that has been left unturned and might need to be uncovered.

- You may want to contact your guidance in the form of an embodiment, an inner guide. This might be someone you know, a great being or angel—or it may be an entirely new presence you come to know within. You can take the following steps if you'd like to find your inner guide:

  - Relax by paying attention to your breathing and counting down from 25 to 1. You can simply do this or choose another relaxation process from part 6, (p.151).

  - In your mind's eye, walk up five steps to an inner room. Become comfortable in this room and explore it. An alternative to this is to walk down a forest path to a cave.

  - Either from a door in the room or in the cave, see your guide emerge. It may be a man, woman, child, animal, symbol, a voice or a presence. Accept whatever you experience, and allow your guide to greet you with total love.

- You may have a question you want to ask, or you may just want to listen and experience the guidance and wisdom that comes forth.

- If you're having any specific difficulty in your life, you may want to ask your guide to assist you with that. Your guide can soothe or even remove it and help you to understand it more fully.

- Your guide may also have a gift for you. If that's the case, see what the gift might be, and allow yourself to receive it.

- You may want to ask your guide what his or her or its name might be and how to make contact in the future.

- See if there is anything else to experience, and if not, bring yourself back by counting down from five to one and making your inner voice louder. Suggest to yourself that you will emerge from relaxation feeling energized and inspired.

- If you like, you may want to remain in open-eyed trance and write some wisdom and guidance onto a piece of paper. Let it just come through your arms, into your hands, out your pen and onto the page. Become a vehicle for this writing. Just as a dancer can dance without thought, a musician can play without thought, you can write without thought. Just let it come through. You may want to pose a question, or you may just wish to receive guidance. If you receive nothing but relaxation, consider that a very peaceful state to receive. Feel free to invent your experience, as this also comes from the deep imaginal realm.

- See if there is any "trigger word" for stimulating the flow that you can use in future trance writing. It may be that you write "My Dear One" on the top of the page. Or you can write a greeting like, "Hello." You can also write your guide's name.

- Trust that your guidance, whether visual or aural or written—or in any other form, is the voice of your spirit. The voice of spirit will always be uplifting and from the realms of light.

Re-identifying Yourself as a Conscious Being

- Explore how your self-esteem is affected by self-images created from your childhood, adolescence, adulthood or any other life experiences.

- Look at how these are frozen pictures from the past and are no longer current.

- Explore your true nature as a divine and radiant being. See how you can re-identify yourself in specific experiences of your life. How might you re-understand your identity in relationships? In your work? In your creative processes? Explore this in as much detail as possible, and see how you might create a new picture of your life. Take a look at what new types of experiences might flow from this enlightened understanding of your true nature.

Working with Healing Light

- After you have explored an issue as fully as possible and you have experienced some release, imagine a beam like that of a flashlight emanating from the universe, bringing love and healing to you. Now imagine that light is emanating from you also, from every pore and from your heart, nurturing and healing every part of you.

- Imagine the light surrounding a particular incident that needs healing, such as a difficult childhood experience. In this case, the light can dissolve the difficulty. You may want to put the healing light around your entire childhood or another era in your life.

- Not only can you send the light into the past, but you can also project it into the future. Surround yourself with light as you experience some new event of your life.

- Protect yourself with the light from any unwanted inner or outer influence, and send off any interference.

- If you're working with the bodymind to heal any ailments or ills, suggest that the light come to you in various forms, such as:

  - *a laser*

    You can use this concentrated form of light to beam on a tumor or any part of your bodymind in need of transformation.

- *streaming rays like sunbeams from the universe*

  Imagine sitting or lying down in the sun, taking in the healing beams.

- *a healing room of light*

  Enter a healing room that has light beams that radiate from the walls, floor, and ceiling. This room has the capacity to heal anyone who enters.

- *a whirling golden ball*

  This golden ball begins at the top of the head and proceeds downward, cleansing all of the chakras or energy centers.

- *a ray from the palm of your hand*

  Experience a beam of light emanating from your hand; touch an ailing part, and experience how healing takes place, as there is, in truth, light emanating from our beings at all times.

- *a beam of light from the center of your forehead*

  Imagine a beam emanating from your third eye bringing increased wisdom and insight.

- In all of your excursions into the inner world of healing, you can adopt a prayerful attitude. This is one that makes a connection with divine guidance, opens to give and receive both knowledge and love, and comes from a state of gratitude for what is already received and what is to be received.

- You can say a prayer before you begin. You can write your own or you can use a universal prayer, some of which are included below.

- One way to create a brief prayer is to say, "I give thanks for..." This can be something that you already have or something that you're manifesting. ("I give thanks for my perfect work." Or "I give thanks for my perfect healing.")

- Your prayer can be one of supplication, of gratitude, or of divine connection ("I Am That").

- Here are some universal prayers that you can include at any point in your own healing work:

1. *Hindu Prayer for Peace*

Oh God, lead us from the unreal to the Real. Oh God, lead us from darkness to light. Oh God, lead us from death to immortality. Shanti, Shanti, Shanti unto all. Oh Lord God almighty, may there be peace in celestial regions. May there be peace on earth. May the waters be appeasing. May herbs be wholesome, and may trees and plants bring peace to all. May all beneficent beings bring peace to us. May all things be a source of peace to us. And may thy peace itself, bestow peace on all, and may that peace come to me also.

2. *Buddhist Prayer for Peace*

May all beings everywhere plagued with sufferings of body and mind quickly be freed from their illnesses. May those frightened cease to be afraid, and may those bound be free. May the powerless find power, and may people think of befriending one another. May those who find themselves in trackless, fearful wildernesses—the children, the aged, the unprotected—be guarded by beneficent celestials, and may they swiftly attain Buddhahood.

3. *Jainist Prayer for Peace*

Peace and Universal Love is the essence of the Gospel preached by all the Enlightened Ones. The Lord has preached that equanimity is the Dharma. Forgive do I creatures all, and let all creatures Forgive me. Unto all have I amity, and unto none enmity. Know that violence is the root cause of all miseries in the world. Violence, in fact, is the knot of bondage. "Do not injure any living being." This is the eternal, perennial, and unalterable way of spiritual life. A weapon, howsoever powerful it may be, can always be superseded by a superior one; but no weapon can, however, be superior to non-violence and love.

4. *Muslim Prayer for Peace*

In the name of Allah, the beneficent, the merciful, praise be to the Lord of the Universe who has created us and made us into tribes and nations, that we may know each other, not that we may despise each other. If the enemy incline towards peace, do thou also incline towards peace, and trust in God, for the Lord is the one that heareth and knoweth all things. And the servants of God, Most Gracious are those who walk on the Earth in humility, and when we address them, we say "PEACE."

5. *Sikh Prayer for Peace*

God adjudges us according to our deeds, not the coat that we wear: that Truth is above everything, but higher still is truthful living. "Know that we attaineth God when we loveth, and only that victory endures in consequence of which no one is defeated."

6. Bahai' Prayer for Peace

Be generous in prosperity, and thankful in adversity.
Be fair in thy judgment, and guarded in thy speech.
Be a lamp unto those who walk in darkness, and a
home to the stranger.
Be eyes to the blind, and a guiding light unto the
feet of the erring.
Be a breath of life to the body of humankind, a dew
to the soil of the human heart, and a fruit upon the
tree of humility.

7. Shinto Prayer for Peace

Although the people living across the ocean
surrounding us, I believe, are all our brothers and
sisters, why are there constant troubles in this
world? Why do winds and waves rise in the ocean
surrounding us? I only earnestly wish that the wind
will soon puff away all the clouds which are
hanging over the tops of the mountains.

8. Native African Prayer for Peace

Almighty God, the Great Thumb we cannot evade
to tie any knot; the Roaring Thunder that splits
mighty trees: the all-seeing Lord up on high who
sees even the footprints of an antelope on a
rockmass here on Earth, You are the one who does

not hesitate to respond to our call. You are the cornerstone of peace.

9. *Native American Prayer for Peace*

O Great Spirit of our Ancestors, I raise my pipe to you. To your messengers the four winds, and to Mother Earth who provides for your children. Give us the wisdom to teach our children to love, to respect, and to be kind to each other so that they may grow with peace in mind. Let us learn to share all the good things that you provide for us on this Earth.

10. *Zoroastrian Prayer for Peace*

We pray to God to eradicate all the misery in the world: that understanding triumph over ignorance, that generosity triumph over indifference, that trust triumph over contempt, and that truth triumph over falsehood.

11. *Jewish Prayer for Peace*

Come let us go up to the mountain of the Lord, that we may walk the paths of the Most High. And we shall beat our swords into ploughshares, and our spears into pruning hooks. Nation shall not lift up sword against nation—neither shall they learn war any more. And none shall be afraid, for the mouth of the Lord of Hosts has spoken.

12. *Christian Prayer for Peace*

Blessed are the peacemakers, for they shall be known as the Children of God. But I say to you that hear, love your enemies, do good to those who hate you, bless those who curse you, pray for those who abuse you. To those who strike you on the cheek, offer the other also, and from those who take away your cloak, do not withhold your coat as well. Give to everyone who begs from you, and of those who take away your goods, do not ask them again. And as you wish that others would do to you, do so to them.[5]

Deepening Your Spiritual Connection

- It's good to establish a discipline that you do at a specific time daily. This is a way for you to experience transcendent realms, to be with yourself, to remember your center.

- If you like, you can create your own daily practice. It may consist of tapping on your meridian points to clear your mind and emotions so that you can meditate, and then stilling your mind with meditation. (See the exercise in this section.) It may include physical movement, such as yoga or t'ai chi or whatever you feel drawn to. You may choose to chant, listen to music, write, or read inspirational books.

- It's good to experience Source during the day, through meditation or music or whatever reminders you create for yourself.

- Healing processes also keep you in touch with your divine essence.

Part Six

Techniques for Transformational Healing

Four Phases of a Healing Session

Phase One

Rapport,
Interview,
Counseling,
Listening

Phase Two

Energy
Therapy

Phase Three

3 STAGES
Experience, Release & Transform

Deep
Inner
Healing

Phase Four

Tape
Making

Phase One

Rapport, Interview, Active Listening, Intuitive Counseling

There are some powerful ways to begin.

Before you do a deep relaxation process, it's good to establish rapport with your client. (The word "client" is used throughout. This, however, may not necessarily be a professional relationship. It can refer to anyone with whom you are working in a healing process. We also refer to your "client" as "she" or "her." This is just for convenience, as either gender can derive benefit from this work.) So, in this process of creating rapport, you listen well, ask leading questions, use your intuition, and guide your client to look deeply into her issues. People love to be heard, and you can listen carefully and deeply to whatever she is telling you. Some typical questions you may ask are:

- How long has this been happening?

- What was going on when this started?

- What are the full details of that experience?

- How is this affecting you now?

- How often has this recurred?

- Did anyone in your family feel the same way?

- What would you like to do instead of this?

- What would you like to accomplish today?

- What would it be like for you to have accomplished this?

As you play your hunches, you find yourself asking questions that are prompted by your intuition. Some of these questions might sound like:

- Did your mother experience this also?

- Did something happen when you were young that felt just like what you're going through now?

- Did you ever feel you've known this person before?

As you listen to the intuitive prompting that comes through you, you'll be guided about what to ask. It's often good to phrase your intuitive hunches as questions so that you can receive confirmation of their validity.

ReSourcing is a rapid process for finding out what saboteurs might be in the way.

Specific techniques can help you to understand how to get to the source of a client's predicament or life challenge. Before you even begin the deep relaxation process, you can get quickly to her saboteurs, the forces that are holding her back. This amazingly rapid and revealing process is called ReSourcing. Your client may say, "I want to lose weight" or "I want to get rid of my pain" or I want to get rid of this problem with a relationship" or "I want to stop smoking." Still there may be many internal factors holding your client back. These are internal saboteurs (also called "psychological reversal").

These resistances to change are not really bad. They're present for a reason. Perhaps the reluctance to change is what your client feels is keeping her safe. She may feel a need for internal protection, though she may not be aware of it. Perhaps there are some character traits or skills she's been developing to get her ready for change, and so the change has been slow to come. Perhaps she's had some very difficult life experiences that she's not resolved, and the situation she thinks she wants to change has actually been her way of creating a smokescreen or a padding or a life raft in the face of these difficult life situations. What you want to do is to find out what's really going on. If you know what's behind her previous inability to change, you can help her find an alternative way or ways of getting these internal needs met. Then you're not pulling the rug out from under her by taking away her protection.

You might say to her, "I'm going to begin a sentence, and I'd like you to finish it. Please don't think about the answer. Just answer from the top of your head. Just say whatever comes to you." You then take her issue and turn it into a negative statement.

You say to her, "What I'm going to say may sound a bit negative, but just go along with it, if you will. Just finish this sentence, 'I don't want to stop smoking because…' Or, 'I don't want to give up this pain in my body or my relationship because…' "

She may then say, "I don't want to give up smoking because it makes me feel better."

And you say, "And I need to feel better because…"

She may respond, "Because it makes me feel safe."

And you say, "And I need to feel safe because…"

And here you get down to the bottom line, the insecurity or need for love. You keep the question going and get more and more information until you feel satisfied that you've gotten to the bottom of things.

Or it might sound like this: "I don't want to give up this relationship because I'm afraid of going out into the world…. I'm afraid of going out into the world because it's scary out there…. I don't think I can handle the world because I'm not okay."

This brings us to a major stumbling block: self-esteem, need for nurturing. These basic issues are often at the heart of every stumbling block in your client's life. It's essential to understand this because when you get to the basic issues, you're able to do healing at the most fundamental level.

It's much like preparing a surface for the spiritual energy to come through. It's priming the pump, removing the barriers so that true healing can take place.

One more illustration. Perhaps you're working with someone who's being beaten by her husband. You can use the ReSourcing technique:

"I don't want to give up my beating because…"

"Because it's what I'm used to. It's the way I've always been treated."

By knowing this you're able to assist her to find the root of her issues, to experience, release and transform them and to come ultimately to the infinite source of love and healing.

You're finding the part of self that is hanging onto the behavior or circumstance or attitude, and in identifying it, you're able to help get needs met in other ways. ReSourcing is a powerful technique that gets very quickly to the saboteurs.

Phase Two

Energy Therapy

Energy therapy can be done both before and during deep healing sessions.

If you do energy therapy before a deep healing session, you locate a symptom or belief or experience that is measurable, and you bring down the intensity with tapping (p. 214). When you've done that, you're ready to do the deep relaxation process.

If you're doing energy therapy when your client is in a deep state, you may want to do most of the tapping for your client. You just work with what she's experiencing, and you help her to release it. You can use the basic tapping technique or the Root Cause Technique (p. 234). Both of these approaches begin with "Even though I have this deep sadness or anger or fear…, etc." This will help her to both release and reframe her experience.

See the section on release techniques (stage two of "experience, release and transform," p. 173) for more details on using energy therapy while your client is deeply relaxed.

Phase Three

Deep Inner Healing

You can induce states of deep relaxation.

There are many types of inductions or relaxation processes. Some of these inductions require another person to facilitate them; others you can do on your own. You may be familiar with visualization or progressive relaxation (relaxing all the parts of the body). There is a dynamic form of relaxation that uses touch and surprise called the rapid induction.

It's good to preface your inductions with the following: "Some people go very deeply; some go very lightly. Most people are in the middle. No matter how deeply you go, you'll still have full awareness and full control—and you'll get the results you need." This is very reassuring to people, as there is a great range of relaxation depth. It is good to reassure the person you're working with that depth of trance is a continuum, that there's no right or wrong way to do this and that she will maintain awareness and control. This is important to many people.

The Rapid Induction

This is a powerful, yet gentle induction that works with the elements of touch and surprise. In those moments of surprise, there is little or no thought. The mind just stops for that brief space in time. This is your opportunity to reach in and help to create a state of deep relaxation.

This technique not only uses surprise; it also uses touch. What you're doing, in essence, is putting the body in a state of deep relaxation with your hands, almost as if you were sculpting it.

Before you use this technique, it's good to have created rapport with your client. You may have had a healing conversation with her, found out what she needs and any other important information, and you are now ready for the next stage of the process. You create good eye contact, and you say, "I'm going to do some 'touch relaxation' (or 'touch hypnosis') with you. I'm going to touch your forehead, your chin, your shoulders, hands, and knees. I may snap my fingers or touch your forehead suddenly. Is this okay with you?" Permission is very important when you're using any kind of touch.

After you've received permission, you proceed to do the following:

- Say, "I'm going to hold up your arm now. Just let it be nice and loose and limp." You hold the arm by the wrist. It can be either arm, and you hold it with your dominant hand.

- At the same time, hold your other hand just above your client's line of vision, ready to snap your fingers. Position your hand just high up enough so that she looks upward slightly—looking upward toward "heaven" or higher consciousness states. Make sure it's not too high, or her neck will be strained, not too close or too low—but just right.

- Then you say, "Take a look at my hand, let your arm be nice and loose and limp, and take a good deep breath in." You take a deep breath in too, and raise her arm a bit—the one you're holding by the wrist.

- You then snap the fingers you're holding above her eyes and release her arm that you're holding by the wrist simultaneously. This will create a state of surprise. (This can also cause a few clients to laugh. This is a reaction to the surprise element and also a release from tension. If this happens, just allow it, and keep on with the process.)

- Take the hand you used to snap with, and touch her on the forehead—not too hard or too soft, but with certainty and gentleness at the same time. While doing this, you say the word, "Sleep!" Of course you know you're not inducing normal sleep, but the word has its own kind of relaxing power. At this point, she will usually close her eyes quite automatically. If she doesn't, you can take your hand and gently bring it down over her eyes to close them. Or you can say, "Just let your eyes close down now."

- Then you take your dominant hand, and cup her chin gently. Say, "Just let your jaw relax." It's important not to force the jaw to relax. Just hold it in your hands, and if there's still tension, say, "Just let your mouth fall open for a moment, and let your jaw completely relax." It's good to say, "That's wonderful" when that happens.

- You then put your hands on her shoulders. Use a loving touch, pressing down slowly, while saying, "Touching your shoulders now. Letting them completely relax." Make sure you honor her body by not pressing too hard. Be firm, but gentle; find a middle ground.

- Then you press her hands, saying, "Touching your hands; relaxing them."

- Then her knees: "Touching your knees; relaxing them."

- You may then touch her forehead again: "Touching your forehead. Just let yourself go more deeply now."

- Now take her arm by the wrist again and say, "Just let your arm be very loose and limp." It probably is very limp by this time anyway. You raise her arm up, and you say, "I'm going to lower your arm, and as I do, you'll be able to go much more deeply." As you slowly lower her arm, you count 5-4-3-2-1 very slowly, and when you're done, gently put her arm down.

- You can repeat any of the above movements if you like, returning to the jaw if necessary.

- When you're done, you can ask if she feels the "relaxing energy." Most often, you will get a very drowsy, profoundly relaxed "Yes."

- Now it's time to do some "deepening." For this purpose there are other techniques you can use: chimes, counting, visualization. We'll talk about these.

There are ways of deepening relaxation.

Playing Chimes

Playing chimes very gently has a soothing effect. It also has an ancient feeling of temple bells, and it calls your clients into deep states of relaxation. You can speak to your client as you play the chimes. "Just pay attention to your breathing now, listening to the sound of the chimes, allowing these sounds to carry you very deeply inside."

Counting

Counting numbers downward has a powerfully relaxing effect. It's non-cognitive, nothing to think about. It's very basic and, in a way, primitive, as it asks nothing of the intellect. You can count from twenty-five down to one, if you like. Do it very slowly, gliding into a state of deep relaxation yourself as you count. You may be able to see your own guide or teacher who comes to give blessings to this session. You can visualize if you like; or just pay attention to the numbers or to your inner energy. You count very slowly, inducing relaxation both with the numbers themselves, and the sound of your voice. If your voice is extraordinarily relaxed, you will send that message across to your client. As you, too, relax, you also transmit that quality of energy. She can feel in a subliminal way just where you're coming from, and the relaxation will deepen profoundly. You can speak in between the numbers or you can just let the numbers speak for themselves. If you do speak, you can say phrases like, "Relaxing more and more deeply—going even more deeply now—very, very relaxed."

You can also take the client even deeper with more numbers. For instance, you can say, "I'm going to count from five to one, and as I do you'll be able to double (or triple) your relaxation. Relaxation starting to double now... doubling more and more... totally relaxed... going to the deepest states of relaxation...."

❋ Checking in with Your Client

At various intervals, you want to check in and see how your client is doing. You can observe the signs of relaxation (see the following page). You can ask questions, such as, "Do you feel that relaxation now?" or "On a scale of one to ten, with ten being the most deeply relaxed, how relaxed would you say you are right now?" Listen to the way the answers are given. If your client's voice is soft, and talking takes some effort, you know that she is very deep. You can also say, "If you feel the relaxation, just nod your head."

Signs of Relaxation

- *Voice is soft.*

  If your client's voice is the same as it would normally be, she is probably in a light state. As already mentioned, there is a marked difference in voice tone when a client is very relaxed.

- *Breathing is slow and deep.*

  Become attuned to your client's breathing process. It will tell you a lot. If deep emotions are coming forth, she may be breathing rapidly from her upper chest. If your client is relaxed, her breathing will be relaxed.

- *Facial features may seem to droop.*

  If you look at the face, you'll most likely see a very relaxed jaw mouth, and cheeks. This is also called the "hypnotic mask"—which we help to create with our hands when we do the rapid induction. We say, "I'm going to touch your jaw now, and you can just let it release and relax. Now let all the muscles of your entire body release and become completely relaxed all the way down your body."

- *There may be a tremor of the closed eyelids.*

  This is a natural and normal reaction that happens to some people as they become deeply relaxed. Some clients become concerned about it, so you can reassure them by saying, "Your eyelids are fluttering now. This is a very good sign, a sign of deep relaxation. It means your body and mind are relaxing very well."

- *Tears may flow from the eyes.*

  This can happen spontaneously when the eyes relax, without any ostensible emotional release. Some people like to have their tears wiped with tissues; others like to allow tears to flow down their face. You can be sensitive to your client's preference—or you can simply ask.

- *Muscles become profoundly relaxed.*

  This is an observable factor, and you can aid this by verbally suggesting that they do so. You can also hold up your client's arm and say, "Just let your arm become loose and limp like a rag doll." You might then release her arm, letting it fall to her lap, suggesting deep muscle relaxation. You can also push gently on the shoulders, suggesting that as you do this, every muscle and nerve, every thought and feeling, every part of your body, will completely relax.

- *You can ask your client.*

  As mentioned above, you can say, "On a scale of one to ten, with ten being the most deeply relaxed, how relaxed would you say you are right now?" Or you can ask your client to nod if she feels ready.

A few words on depth of relaxation:

Relaxation states can be gauged on a continuum. There are the deepest states, sometimes called the somnambulistic or even the coma states or the ultra-depth states. There are the very light states, sometimes called the hypnoidal states. And there are states in between. Most people are between the two extremes. Your client can have healing results in any of these states, and that's why it is important to point out, as mentioned before, that results can be obtained in any of these states of relaxation. You say to your client, "Some people go very deeply. Some go very lightly. Most people are in the middle. You still have full awareness and full control, and you'll get the results you need." This is very important to mention, as some people have the expectation that they'll go instantly into the deepest states. Since this is not necessarily the case, let them know that there is a wide range of possible depth states and that their needs can be met in any of them.

❊ Deepening through Visualization

Many people use visualization to create deep relaxation states. The possibilities are as infinite as your own imagination. Here are just a few:

- Imagine a wave of relaxing energy that washes over your body and mind from your head to your feet, just like a waterfall.

- Visualize a beautiful, relaxing place. See yourself there, totally at ease.

- Imagine a small child throwing stones into a pond, and see the concentric circles made by the splash. Do this several times, and tell yourself to relax more and more.

- Relax your body, part by part, starting either at the bottom of your feet or the top of your head.

- Imagine that you're floating on a cloud.

- Imagine a candle inside of you, the light of which grows into a beautiful expansive glow.

The possibilities go on and on. Two important points about using visualization: It's important to remember that not everyone is visual. You can say, "You'll be able to see or feel or hear or just get an impression." This way, all modalities are included. Another important point about visualization is that it is essentially a cognitive experience. This is why sometimes it's even more effective to use the rapid induction, which goes beyond mental activity, or counting, which is a more primitive function than visualization. You can include visualization with all forms of induction, as it has its own significant place in the field of deep relaxation.

Checking to See if Your Client is Ready to Begin

You can ask, "Are you ready to begin?" Or you can say, "On a scale of one to ten, with ten being the most relaxed, how relaxed would you say you are right now?" If you feel you need to deepen the relaxation, go ahead and do that. If your client is ready, you can now begin.

❧

Remember the three stages of an inner healing session.

You will find yourself moving through the three stages of experience, release and transform as you work. In the first stage, your client experiences what she needs to know or feel about her own process. Then comes the release. Next comes the transformation into higher consciousness. It's not always a neat progression from stage to stage, though it usually takes this form. Sometimes release is contained in the first stage of "experiencing." Sometimes transformation comes right at the beginning, when a client is ready to see and understand her life from a new point of view. Still the guidelines of experience, release, and transform will give you a structure for doing this work. If you keep this in mind, you will get a sense of where your sessions are going moment by moment.

Please note: You'll find some of the same material in the next section that you've seen in other parts of this book. It has been re-stated for emphasis and for ease of use.

The Three Stages of
Transformational Healing

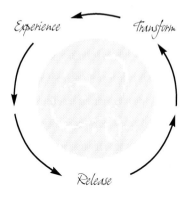

Experience ← Transform

Release

Experience

- *Explore, Discover, Feel*

  "Let's see what your deep inner mind would like to pay attention to today." Then you explore it, experience pictures, thoughts, beliefs, impressions and/or feelings about it.

- *Find the Root Cause*

  "Let's see what might have been the roots of the issue you're experiencing today."

  Root Causes: Separation, attachment, abandonment, womb/birth, family of origin parents' wounds, past lives, subpersonalities/fragments, traumas, entities, tendencies of the mind/*samskaras*, karma and destiny, socioeconomics.

Release

Express, balloons, energy therapies, visualizations, arm pull/cosmic vacuum, pull out cords, just let go.

Transform

Love, comfort and compassion; guidance and
wisdom; strong part assist other part; transform
imagery; witness: float above, see screen, stand on
mountaintop, stand back. Find soul lessons; reframe;
healing light and water; suggestions, affirmations,
triggers, anchors, tape.

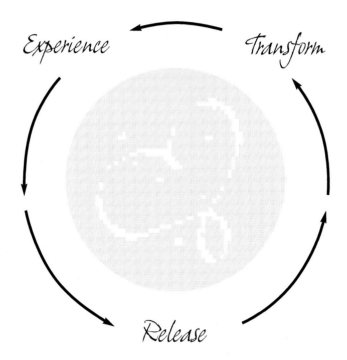

Experience

Transform

Release

Stage One:
Experience

*There are effective words to say to begin an
inner healing process.*

Here are some effective ways to begin your inner
healing. After you've completed your induction, you can
ask, "Are you ready to begin?" If you like, you can ask your
client, "On a scale of one to ten, with ten being the most
deeply relaxed, how relaxed would you say you are right
now?" When you feel she's ready, you can say the
following:

- *Giving directions to your client*

  "I'm going to count from three to one, and when I
  get to one, I'm going to snap my fingers gently and
  touch you lightly on your shoulder like this (snap
  gently and touch). This will be a signal to your deep
  inner mind to show you whatever it is that you
  want or need to pay attention to today."

  This is an important way of phrasing your
  directions: "… whatever it is that you want or need
  to pay attention to today." This direction assumes,

and rightly so, that the deep inner mind is quite brilliant and will take your client and your session to whatever place she needs to go. It opens the doors to anything that might come forth that is relevant to the healing process.

Another way of phrasing this might be, "Your deep inner mind will take you to the root of your issue." (You can state the issue.) Or you can say, "… to whatever is in need of healing."

- *Making certain that you cover all the modalities*

  Then you tell your client: "You may see this as a picture or feel it or think about it or just have an impression. However you experience it is just fine. So just let yourself see or feel or hear or know whatever it is that your deep inner mind would like to pay attention to today."

  This will cover all the various ways of experiencing.

- *Experiencing her experience*

  You then count from three to one, snap your fingers gently, touch her shoulder lightly and again mention the various possible ways she can experience (seeing, feeling, thinking, and getting an impression).

  After you do this, you can say, "You can share with me what you're experiencing now." If she says she's experiencing nothing, you can ask, "If you could experience something, what might it be?" or "What is that nothing like?"

You listen carefully, knowing that it is your job to be the midwife of the experience more than the director. Sometimes you will need to be more directive, though it is good to allow your client to see what's inside and explore it fully.

- *Vivifying her experience*

  When something comes forth, a picture of something, a feeling either in the physical or the emotional body, a thought, an impression, your job is to bring it to life. This means that you find out the details, ask the right questions, and guide your client to vivify and enliven the experience so that you can open it up for healing and transformation.

  When the experience is open, use your intuition to see where to guide it. Make certain you don't lead it where you want to go—but where your client wants and needs to be. Allow the client's own process to unfold naturally. You want to avoid over-leading.

- *Asking the right questions*

  Here are some questions you can ask while your client is in a deep state of relaxation:

  - What's happening now?

  - Tell me about it.

- Where do you feel it in your body?

- Can you describe it?

- Tell me more.

- Who is it that's experiencing this?

- How old are you?

- Where are you?

- Is anyone else there?

- If this (feeling, part of you, quality) could speak, what would it say?

- What does it look like?

- What's happening now?

- Is it moving or changing in any way?

- If you could experience that, what might it be?

- What does that part need?

- What is that here to teach you?

Notice that toward the end of these questions, there is a different quality. As soon as you ask "What does that part need?"—you are entering the transformational stage. Usually that part needs comfort, love and awareness. We'll talk about how to handle that later.

Your contribution to the session consists of asking the right questions, not over-leading, but eliciting from your client what is important for her experience. If you can "get into" this process, use your imagination, participate fully in it, you will do great work. Allow yourself to explore your client's experience at the same time as she's exploring it. You don't take it on as your own, but you allow yourself to understand it enough to ask one good question after another. You may see where something is going, and you may want to lead it. Sometimes this is appropriate, especially if your client needs more prompting, but if you allow the experience to unfold from within her, her deep inner mind will brilliantly provide all that is needed. Sometimes what you think she should experience is different from what her own inner wisdom wants to show her. Listening to your client is an art form. You are not superimposing your ideas on her. You are listening carefully and actively, standing back enough to allow her own process to unfold. You do step in where needed, though you are the servant of the process. You are not the doer.

Remember that this first stage of the inner healing process can take your client to any of the root causes of human suffering: attachment, abandonment, traumas, fears, other lifetimes, parents' wounds, womb and birth issues, unwanted energies, tendencies of the mind, subpersonalities and more. You are a vehicle for holding the space so that your client can come to know the important issues of her life.

It's also good to keep your questions in the present tense. You say, "What is happening?" Not "What was happening?" You want your client to have as vivid an experience as possible. The past tense implies that this is a memory. The present tense brings the experience to life so that it is open for healing.

After you ask the questions, you'll find that there is a moment in which it is time for the session to move into the release and experience stages. You'll come to know when that is. You want to allow for the experience to take place; yet you don't want it to drag on incessantly. It usually has its own time factors. It is a natural unfoldment of "experience, release and transform."

After your client has brought forth her pictures, feelings, thoughts, and impressions—then release and transformation of consciousness take place as a beautiful flow, a result of this profound paying of attention to what is there. You're trusting that there is a guidance system in both you and your client that is waiting to be called upon. This is the great work of inner healing. We are assisting in a great universal transformational process in which darkness becomes light. We are bringing forth our highest qualities of love, wisdom and enlightenment. This is what we came to this earth to know. We will look at "release and transformation" in greater detail ahead.

- *Steps you can take if clients don't seem to be "getting anything"*

  If you find that "nothing" is happening for your client, you can say the following:

  - "If you did experience something, what might it be?"

  - Or you can say, "I'm going to hold up your arm and release it onto your lap. As I do this, the experience will come right to you. You'll be able to see or feel or hear or know it."

  - Or you can say, "What's that nothing like? Tell me about it."

  - You can also say, "What are you experiencing in your body (or your emotions) right now." You can begin there. You can also become more directive, "Let's go to a time when you were a child experiencing this." Or "Let's go to the source of your____(name the issue)."

  - You can also say, "Use your imagination. Pretend you know."

  - Or "What is coming to you now?" If it's darkness, explore the darkness. If it's tension, get into it. Find out what qualities it has.

  Just get into what's going on. Whatever's coming up is the issue and needs to be explored. In this sense, there is no such thing as resistance. Whatever is there is the material for your session.

Stage Two:
Release

*There are powerful techniques you can
use for releasing.*

After you've completed the first stage of the inner
healing process, the experiencing phase, you're ready to
guide your client to the next stage of releasing. It's a
matter of careful timing to know just when to move your
client into this stage. You can assess how completely she
has experienced her experience, and you can also ask her,
"Are you ready to release this now?"

Often release is a natural flow; it happens as a direct
result of having paid careful attention to what is
happening within. Sometimes, however, it requires a
bit of direction.

- ### *Energy therapy as a release technique*

    Not only is energy therapy an excellent tool to use
    prior to a deep healing session, but you can also
    use it as a release technique when issues arise while
    your client is relaxed.

It might look like this:

> Let's say your client has viewed herself as
> "worthless." This may not be how she sees herself in
> totality, but there is a part of her that experiences
> her worthlessness. You may have done some tapping
> with her prior to the relaxation process on these
> feelings of worthlessness.
>
> When she's relaxed she may then experience herself
> as a child who's been put down by her family. She
> says she's the "messed up" one because she's not
> obedient like her sister. The child is sad and alone.
> You may want to do more tapping with her now. It
> may be appropriate for you to do the tapping, as
> her hands are likely to be very relaxed. You can use
> any of the variations. This time, it may be the Root
> Cause Technique (p. 234):
>
> - "Even though I feel sad and alone, I deeply,
>   completely accept myself." You do this three
>   times.
>
> - You tap at the beginning of her eyebrow: "I am
>   eliminating all of the sadness in the deepest
>   root causes of feeling sad and alone."
>
> - Tap under her eye: "I am eliminating all of the
>   fear in the deepest root causes of feeling sad
>   and alone."
>
> - You do the rest of this process as you work on
>   her anger, emotional trauma, shame, guilt, grief,
>   and you then move into forgiveness and
>   reframing, transforming the outcome.

After this is complete and while she remains relaxed, she sees an image of all of her family members giving her love. She imagines that love is also coming to her from God. She feels surrounded with an aura of love and care. She also feels love emanating from within herself.

This is an example of a way in which you can use energy therapy while your client is in the middle of a profound inner healing process.

• *Releasing with balloons*

This method involves using an actual balloon that your client holds in her two hands while in deep relaxation. As she is experiencing the fear, anger, trauma or deep experience and is ready to release it, you can say, "Would you like to work with an actual balloon to help release this?" It is important to get her permission. If she says "no," just go onto another technique. If she says that she'd like to do it, then tell her that you're going to blow up a few balloons for her to use. You blow them up (practicing your technique in advance so that you have ease with blowing up and tying the balloons as gracefully as possible). Then you give her one and say, " Just go ahead and hold it in your hands and press your thumbs and fingers into it as hard as you'd like. If you'd like to express something, say something to _____, just feel free to say whatever you'd like." At this point, she can speak up to any family member or perpetrator, to express what has long been withheld. So she may say, "Dad, your behavior has hurt me and the family, and I want to say this to you." This helps her to relieve an emotional burden that may have been hanging on for many years.

You encourage her to press even harder into the balloon until it finally bursts. At this point your client feels a profound release. And yes, she stays relaxed—even more relaxed and relieved now.

Just make certain you get her permission to use this technique. It's powerful and effective. It has been adapted from the work of Roger LaChance as a part of his Emotional Release Technique and allows clients to release emotions such as anger and fear in a powerful way. It has been said that this technique actually moves these emotions out of the nervous system. It uses surprise and sound to shift long-held emotional issues.

• Arm Pull and Cosmic Vacuum

This is a very physical and graphic release technique that employs touch and sound. When your client is ready to release, you say to him or her, "I'm going to hold your arm up now, and I'm going to pull on it and make some whooshing sounds. Is that all right with you?" If it is all right, then you pull on her outstretched arm, as you make the whooshing sounds and encourage her to let go of whatever needs to be released.

Then you position your hands several inches from her body (over her aura), and you proceed to clear each one of her chakras or energy centers with clockwise hand movements, beginning at the top of her head. As you do this, you make more whooshing noises and clockwise hand movements, aligning her chakras with sound and movement. You can tell her what you're doing. You can also pull off "old energy" as you do this, shaking off your hands as you work, clearing the old energy out of her energy field.

Then you smooth out her energy, making gentle sounds now that resemble a mild breeze. You use your hand to travel over her auric field, and you may want to say to her, "We're bringing in light and healing now. How does that feel?"

- *Pulling out cords*

  You and your client may also wish to pull out cords of outworn relationships or issues. These are energetic connections that have been binding her and that she is ready to release. You can discuss this with her and ask her if she wishes to release the bind. Then you can find an energy center that feels important to you—usually the heart center or solar plexus near the stomach. You can, if it feels comfortable to you, pull gently on your clients clothing and "pull out" the cord. You ask her to also be a part of this process, envisioning the release within.

  Next you can bring light to the areas that have been released, smoothing them out, and filling them with healing love.

Some clients are ready to release, and others are not. If not, this may mean that there is more learning to receive from their difficulties. Also release may happen in layers or increments. We always keep it in mind that "healing is the work of a lifetime" and that life issues are the curriculum of this very profound school of inner education.

There is a spiral or circular effect in experiencing, releasing and transforming. The process keeps moving on. The issues become easier to understand and to release as the spiral moves upward and as we do our "om-work." This is the important work that we've come here to do.

Stage Three:
Transform

*Transformation is the movement
from suffering into higher consciousness,
a state of ultimate healing.*

This movement into higher consciousness can take a
number of forms:

- Love

- Compassion

- Forgiveness

- Wisdom

- Witness Consciousness

- Light

- Peace

Sometimes in a healing session, this movement of
consciousness happens naturally as a direct result of
focusing awareness on the original difficulty. There are
also ways to facilitate this process. We'll look at specific

ways in which you can open the vistas for your clients to have these higher healing experiences.

The transformational stage comes after you've fully experienced and released the original issue. Some clients are ready to begin here. They may want only to experience inner guidance or some other aspect of transformation. Also, the transformational state may be that which serves as a release for the original issue; forgiveness, for example, may be the release for anger.

So now let's see some ways to facilitate the movement into grace.

- *Love*

  All of our clients have the capacity to heal their lives with love. Healing love can lift up and unify all fragments of self, to overcome all the dark places within. Someone once said that the lack of love is the root of 90% of the problems of human existence. As a healer, you can be a vehicle through which your clients can come back to love. You can, yourself, be loving to your clients—in the highest sense of the word. You can assist them to experience their own love. And you can be a channel through which transcendent love can come forth. Healing love can take many forms—from the human to the Divine. Here are some of the ways that it can be experienced:

    - You can ask your client if she'd like to hold a part of the self that is in need of healing. You may want to give her a pillow or something soft to hold.

- You can ask her if she'd like to change a picture or a scenario to a more loving picture.

- You can ask her how she'd like to soothe or bring comfort to the troubled part of herself. This opens the way for her to bring in her own form of love and comfort. It may take the form of a grandparent, a trusted friend, a specific angelic presence, a loving animal, a great being, a part of herself that is especially loving, or it may be the love of God. She may be able to get in touch with a radiant aspect of herself that has the ability to heal all other parts.

- You can explore the energetic aspect of love and see how it feels in your client's heart center. See if there's any tension or if there's the feeling of a wall, and find out what might be needed to open it. She may want to imagine a light emanating from her heart center, or she may find that by experiencing what's there, an opening happens spontaneously.

- She may be able to experience loving messages from within. You can ask her if there may be a wise and loving part of herself that wishes to speak to her.

- She may be able to experience a more abstract form of universal love. It may be an energy emanating from the universe and penetrating her heart center, filling up her being. It may also emanate from inside of her, circulating throughout her being and filling her with divine love.

- It may take the form of gratitude, and she can feel grateful for all she's experienced, as it is all a part of her evolutionary path.

- *Compassion*

  Compassion is the deep awareness of the suffering of another, coupled with the wish to relieve it. The work of the healer is not only to have compassion for the trials that clients are going through, but also to help foster clients' own compassion as an important part of their healing process. Here are some ways that you can serve as a vehicle for the experience of compassion:

  - You can assist her to experience compassion for the hurt parts of herself. Instead of rejecting them or pushing them away, she can bring in love and healing to the three-year old or teen or inner addict or overeater.

  - She can also have ultimate compassion for those who've wounded her. This is, of course, a process, and she may first need to experience her indignation or rage or sadness and then move toward compassion. She can then see that everyone is suffering—including perpetrators. She can be invited to experience the childhood of a perpetrator or take a look into his or her psyche. She may want to stand on top of a mountain to gain perspective on the difficulties or life lessons that person might be going through. She can then experience his or her higher self in order to heal the darkness.

- She may be able to experience a compassionate being, a great teacher or healer or even someone she knows. She can experience how this one might view her life and how he or she might heal her.

- She can see how the universe, itself, is transforming her through whatever difficulties she is undergoing, and she can experience the compassion in a much larger sense. She can see how the difficult issues of her life have been the fuel for her to become strong and great.

- *Forgiveness*

Forgiveness is an uplifted state in which all negativities are released. It can come after deep inner healing. It may be the direct result of compassion for the suffering of a perpetrator. It may be the result of seeing that there is a great plan at work, and perhaps destiny has played a part in the situation. It may come after seeing that each player in the drama has been doing the best he or she can do according to his or her level of understanding. It may arise after seeing the toll that carrying hatred or grudges or resentment can take.

It may come from an uplifted view in which all negativity simply melts away. It's good for healers to remember that not everyone is ready to forgive quickly. Some people need to come to know their deep feelings and move through them step by step.

- Your client may want to experience each person in her "cast of characters" and see how the actions of each were the products of their own suffering and ignorance.

- You may want to do the "Root Cause Technique" (p. 234) with her. After moving through sadness, fear, anger, emotional trauma, shame, guilt and grief, there is a tapping point on the index finger and a reframing of her experience in which she forgives everyone involved because "they were only doing the best they knew how to do."

- *Wisdom*

  - Instead of attempting to dazzle clients with your own knowledge, it's of great value to bring forth the innate intelligence, wisdom and knowledge of your clients. The deep inner mind is itself a brilliant mechanism. It will take you where you need to go when you put it on "search mode." You can then ask it to show you the most significant experience that you need to pay attention to or the root of the problem. There is also a higher guidance system inside that your client can experience. There is the intuitive ability that you can bring forth from your client as well. This can show her what was going on in the psyche of a perpetrator or in her mother who may have been unable to give her all the love she needed. Clients can also find lost objects, discover the answer to previous puzzles, and open up a source of knowing within themselves.

- After the "experience, release and transform" process, ask your client what her "wise mind" might tell her about her situation. What has the situation been trying to tell her? What might she need to understand? What might be her next step?

- You can lead your client toward her inner guide by saying the following:

  - "In your mind's eye, walk up five steps to an inner room. Just let yourself explore this room and feel comfortable." (An alternative to this is for her to walk down a forest path to a cave.)

  - "From a door, see your guide emerge. It may be a man, woman, child, animal, symbol, a voice or a presence. Accept whatever you experience, and allow your guide to greet you with total love."

  - "If you have a question, go ahead and ask your guide, or you may just want to listen and experience the guidance and wisdom that comes forth."

- "Your guide may also have a gift for you. If that's the case, see what the gift might be, and allow yourself to receive it."

- "You may want to ask your guide what his or her or its name might be and how to make contact in the future."

- "See if there is anything else to experience with your guide."

- *Witness Consciousness*

  Witness consciousness is a state in which you're able to stand back enough to see the larger picture. It's the ability to be the witness, to see apparent reality from a more panoramic point of view. There are many healing advantages to this. You're able to move to another level of awareness in which you can see the meaning of events. You can see the learning experiences or the blessings. You're able to move to a state of understanding in which emotional issues shift. Abandonment and separation shift into inclusiveness; aloneness shifts to all-oneness. Fear becomes faith as you witness events from a larger point of view. You experience the protection in the universe. You have an expanded sense of wisdom, and you see a larger plan for things. You can assist your clients to come into these expanded witness states that are the next level of their healing processes. Here are some ways you can do this:

- When your client has found an event or experience in her life that has been particularly difficult, and after she has experienced it and released the emotional charge, suggest that she stand back from it enough to see what contributions it has made to the growth of her soul. Some information she might get from this understanding might be:

  - What strengths has she gained from it?

  - How has it led her to her spiritual path?

  - What has it been attempting to teach her?

  - What aspects of her character have transformed because of this experience?

  - How has it opened her to wisdom and compassion for the suffering of all beings?

  - What blessings are contained in the difficulties?

- You can assist her to experience some particular visualizations that will foster witness consciousness. You can say to her "In your mind's eye, imagine that you're standing on a mountaintop or floating above the scenarios of your life or seeing these experiences on a screen. As you look down or onto the screen, you can see people and events from your life in more expanded ways." You can suggest that she then do the following:

- "Observe the childhood of someone in your life. See what life situations have created the kind of person he or she has become."

- "See people from your life as beings working out their issues on the wheel of life. See them from an evolutionary perspective, growing and changing with the life lessons they're receiving."

- You can assist her to call upon any transcendent forces to help her view her situations from the larger perspective. She can invite in her I AM consciousness or highest wisdom or great beings such as Buddha, Christ, Quan Yin, or Moses. She can call to guides or angels to uplift her vision and bring forth a more expanded understanding.

- You can suggest that she find a word or a phrase, an image or a gift that can serve as a reminder of her expanded view. She can put her thumb together with her index finger to further trigger this in the future.

- She may be able to experience the divine energy inherent in all things, to come to know a dimension of consciousness that sees everything as energy. Here the distinctions and sorrows transform into a more ecstatic level of being.

- *Light*

  - Light is a source of great power for healing and transformation. It is an energy so strong and of such high frequency that it can raise the vibration of anything it touches. It can heal childhood difficulties or physical problems; it can protect and purify; it can uplift the emotions and it can transform the experience of both living and dying. Everything is made of particles of light; it's the spiritual substance of the universe, the remedy for the darkness of life on earth. Here are some ways to work with light. Some of these approaches involve suggesting that your client experience the light. Others involve your sending the light as an emanation from and through yourself.

    - After you have explored an issue as fully as possible and your client has experienced some release, you can suggest that there is a beam like that of a flashlight emanating from the universe, bringing love and healing to her. Now imagine that light is emanating from her also, from every pore and from her heart, nurturing and healing every part of her being.

    - You can suggest that the light surround a particular incident that needs healing, such as a difficult childhood experience. In this case, the light can dissolve the difficulty. She may want to put the healing light around her entire childhood or another era in her life.

- Not only can she send the light into the past, but she can also project it into the future. She can surround herself with light as she experiences some new event of her life.

- She can protect herself with the light from any unwanted inner or outer influence, and send off any interference.

- When working with the bodymind to heal any ailments or ills, suggest that the light come to her in various forms, such as:

  - *a laser*
    You can use this concentrated form of light to beam on a tumor or any part of the bodymind in need of healing.

  - *streaming beams like sunbeams from the universe*
    She can imagine sitting or lying down in the sun, healing in the beams of light.

  - *a healing room of light*
    She can enter a healing room that has light beams that radiate from the walls, floor, and ceiling. This room has the capacity to heal anyone who enters.

- *a whirling golden ball*
  This golden ball begins at the top of the head and proceeds downward, cleansing all of the chakras or energy centers.

- *a ray from the palm of your hand*
  You can ask your client to experience a beam of light emanating from your hand, and when you, with her permission, touch an ailing part, healing takes place. Your client can do the same with her own hand, as there is, in truth, light emanating from our beings at all times.

- *a beam from the center of your forehead*
  You can send a beam emanating from your third eye to your client, remembering that as you hold the intention for healing, you set up an environment to facilitate this process.

- *Other healing imagery for states of transformation*

  - *Healing water*
    Your client can imagine that she is bathing in beautiful healing water, just the right temperature and just the right depth. She can bathe away old issues of abuse, physical pains, or unwanted thoughts or energies.

- *Blanket of peace*
  She can imagine that she is surrounded with a comforting blanket of absolute peace.

- *Sanctuary*
  She can experience that she's in a perfectly safe and sacred place that is dedicated to her healing.

Phase Four
Tape Making

You can make original, individual tapes after deep healing sessions.

It's almost always a good idea to make tapes for your clients. It reminds them of what you and they have done in the sessions. It helps them relax and sleep. It's like having daily inner healing. Making a tape is also an excellent way to complete your session. The tape does not need to be long. In fact, a 12-15 minute tape may be easier for your client to find time to listen to than a long one.

The tapes are not difficult to make—especially if you just relax yourself and let them "happen" through you. They consist of an induction and an extended process of suggestions, reframing, restatement of the tools your client will use to make the changes, visualizations, spiritual transformation—and more. Your tape will serve as extended suggestions, and you may find that your clients want to listen to them for months or years.

Let's take a look at what you'll do when making the tape.

❁ The Induction

You've come almost to the end of your session, and you can now re-induce relaxation for the tape. The added advantage for your client is that she can now go even more deeply into relaxation by becoming re-induced. Here's what one induction might sound like. Feel free to use it or to create one of your own. Put on some beautiful music on a nearby player, and say into your microphone:

> *"Just take a nice deep breath in and exhale, and as you do, just let go of any stress or tension. Take another deep breath in and exhale once again, and let a peaceful wave of relaxing energy wash over your body and your mind—just like a waterfall of relaxation from your head all the way down to your feet. Just pay attention to your breathing now—breathing in and relaxing, breathing out and releasing. Your breath coming in and going out like the waves on the ocean— coming in and going out and becoming a part of the ocean. I'm now going to count from twenty-five to one, and as I do, you can go very, very deeply."*

Count backward very slowly—and at this time, you too can go more deeply into relaxation so that you'll be more open to letting the messages flow through you on the tape. You can also do a very brief progressive muscle relaxation at this point—or you can just continue on to the next step.

Movement to Strength, Peace, Higher Self

You are now ready to go to the next stage of the tape, and here comes a turning point. You talk about the fact that because your client is relaxing so deeply; he or she can go to a place of strength, peace, wisdom, and creativity—whatever higher quality your client most needs for his or her particular journey at the time. It might sound like this:

"And when you relax this deeply, you go to a place of great peace inside of you, and you realize that a very powerful change is taking place in your life."

(You mention specifically the change that you've been working on with the client.)

"You know that it is the right time for this change. You've done such good work to make this happen, and you now have all the tools you need. You are now able to make these changes more easily than ever before. You have great support, and you are now ready to…" (…whatever your client is ready to do or be or have).

The Issues Reframed

The main portion of your tape will contain whatever material your own wisdom deems necessary for your client. Here are some possibilities:

- *"You have many good reasons for...."* (Whatever it is that your client may be working on, especially if it has to do with behavioral change or habit control.) You may want to state the reasons positively (e.g., *"Now you can run without getting tired because you've overcome your old patterns."*).

- *"You have all the ability you need to...*(get the job, heal your body, exercise...)."

- *"There are plenty of other things that you can do instead of...* (what you've been doing"—state specifically if you like). Here you can talk about specific behavioral changes that you and your client have discussed. State these specifically. Give your client all the necessary tools. (You can even give a trigger/anchor, *"Whenever you put your thumb together with your index finger and say...* (you will have chosen a specific word or phrase beforehand), *you can feel a great feeling of peace and* (...whatever else is necessary)."

- You can talk about anything that you and your client have either discussed in session or about material that has come up in deep healing—always taking a positive view.

- You can use visualizations. You remember, of course that not everyone is visual, so you offer other options such as thinking about it, feeling it, etc. *"Just imagine yourself looking and feeling the way you'd like..."* or *"Just experience your body as healed and whole."*

- If you absolutely don't know what to say, you can use a script book to give you ideas. You can use parts of scripts if you like, and weave them into your client's special needs.

Spiritual Transformation

Bring in light, healing water, love, Source, wisdom, guides—whatever you're guided to do. Use intuition and knowledge of your client to make certain that you aren't stepping out of your client's accepted frame of reference. You may want to subtly ask about this during the session, for your client may want to meet up with Jesus or Buddha or Mohammed, whatever is best for her.

Ending Your Tape

When you're ready to end, you can say the following:

"All of these ideas are penetrating into your subconscious mind having a powerful effect on you, helping you greatly. And if you're listening to this tape before bedtime, you can just feel free to float off to sleep. You can rest assured that you are relaxing very deeply and that you're having positive results. You listen to this tape on a regular basis, and every time you listen, you'll be able to go more and more deeply. If you're listening to this tape at a time when you'd like to come back, I'm going to count from one to five, and when I

get to five, you'll be able to come back feeling full of life and energy, with a sense of vitality peacefulness and joy. So, coming on back—full of life, full of energy and a wonderful sense of well being, happiness and joy."

Giving the Tape to Your Client

You may want to put a label on your tape, and give it a title. Put it in a tape box, and tell your client to be sure to make a copy of the tape to create a backup "just in case." You can tell your client to listen to it every day, as this will keep him or her in touch with the process. Clients love their tapes. Many of them listen to them regularly, and often listen to them for a long time.

Tapes are a great tool that we have as healers. They can double the effectiveness of our work.

More Tape Techniques

There are other effective healing elements for your tapes.

- *Anchoring the change*

  To "anchor" means "to hold the change in place." It's a term derived from neurolinguistic programming (NLP). One way of anchoring is to ask your client to find a word or phrase that symbolizes her new state. You can then say, "Whenever you put your thumb together with your index finger and you say your word (or phrase), you bring back these positive feelings and experiences." Your client can find this anchor before you make your tape, and you can include it the tape as well.

- *Future-Pacing*

  This is also a term from NLP, and it means that you project into the future and see how life would look once the change is in place. You may use a movie screen, a TV, or a theater. Or you can just ask your client to look in her mind's eye for what may be her next step or to view her change in the future. This is an excellent way to create grounding, a firm foundation for the transformational experience, as it helps your client to see what the change might look like as it is played out in everyday life. This too can be included on the tape.

- *Post-Relaxation Suggestions*

  This form of suggestion, also called "post-hypnotic suggestion," is a positive way of speaking to your client, appealing to her deep inner mind. You might say, for example, "You may find yourself filled with light as you experience the freedom in this next stage of your life."

You can complete your session.

If after a few minutes your client hasn't fully emerged from relaxation, you can say, "Would you like me to help you come back more completely? Okay, I'm going to clap six or seven times in front of your face, and that will bring you right back." Most of the time, you won't need to use this technique, but it does help those who make a slow re-entry.

Using these approaches can help you to facilitate true transformation in the life of anyone who has the opportunity to work with you. It all becomes easier with practice. Just allow the session to unfold; lead gracefully, not too much or too little. Your own wisdom will be your guide.

There are helpful points to remember as you do your healing work.

- *There are essentially four phases to an inner healing session.*

  The first phase is the interview process, which consists of active listening, asking relevant questions, creating rapport and doing intuitive counseling. The second is using energy therapy. The third is deep inner healing and further energy therapy while your client is relaxed. And the fourth is about making a tape for your client.

- ### It's wise to use "permissive language."

  Another word for this is "non-authoritarian." Instead of saying, "I want you to…" (as in "I want you to relax," for example), it's more gentle and palatable for many people if you use other words and phrases, such as:

  > *"You'll be able to…"*

  > *"You may want to…"*

  > *"If you would…"*

  > *"If you like, you can…"*

  > *"Just go ahead and…"*

  > *"Just let yourself…"*

  To some people, this makes a real difference. Some people don't like to be told, "I want you to…"

- ### Your intention makes all the difference in your sessions.

  You are "holding the space" for healing to take place, and your intention that your client will have an experience that is for her highest good will serve her well. You are, of course, a vehicle for the healing power to flow through you, and your intention for this to happen assures that you will be centered into the healing process.

- *Your trust in the subconscious mind and the healing power will guide you in your work.*

  The deep inner mind has a brilliance all its own. You ask it to guide you and your client, and it takes you where you need to be. In your session, you are the "tour guide" rather than the "doer." You hold the space for the infinite wisdom and the data of the subconscious mind to manifest as a healing system for your client. You take responsibility for being present, holding the space, and asking the right questions; yet you are not the doer, and this is a very important ground of being for you.

- *You find your own personal approach.*

  You naturally have your own style of working, which evolves with practice. It's good to allow your intuition, imagination and wisdom to guide you. It's also good to make a strong connection with the Source of all healing, as you call it forth for you and your client.

- *You center yourself for the work.*

  It's important for you to have a regular practice that centers you—meditation or self-hypnosis— something that opens you to the energies of healing and the natural healing abilities in yourself. It may help to do some type of invocation (either silently or aloud) that calls in the higher self of both you and your client, that invokes protection and guidance. Centering yourself in this way is like preparing for a dive off a diving board by making certain that all forces are in alignment, making certain that both feet are on the diving board and that you are concentrating fully. This is how you open as a vehicle for forces larger than yourself to operate in your work. This also helps you to be grounded and centered.

- *Witness consciousness helps you to stand back.*

  As you become more and more proficient at fine-tuning your abilities to stand back and observe your clients' difficulties as experiences from which they need to learn, you are able to be the witness. This state of witness-consciousness gives you the capacity to work with someone and not take on his or her issues. When you play into the situation and over-identify, your ego gets involved, and then you can take on your clients' difficulties. Even if you're working on the same issues, you can assume the witness state. You can learn to stand back and view from a distance. You can also surround yourself with light and ask in prayer for the care of both of you as you work together for the highest good. The fact that you are doing transformational healing work means that you shift into higher consciousness with your client as you work. This transforms the energy of the entire situation and creates a state of healing.

- *It is good to be sensitive to your client.*

  You can watch and listen for signs of your client's needs and attitudes. You are sensitive to her need to feel safe, to be comfortable in the environment, to be informed about what's happening in your session. You can explain everything you're doing, ask if it's okay to touch at specific points, let her know that all is well.

- *It works well to "get into" what's happening in your client's consciousness.*

  Even though you're assuming the state of the witness, you still want to imagine what your client is experiencing. This will help you to ask the right questions, to see what your client is feeling, to see what steps are needed for healing. This is what shamans do; they go there with the client so that they can assist in the healing process. You don't necessarily need to "go there," though it is very good to become highly aware of what's happening at each stage of the process. This can make the difference between good work and great work on your part. Entering your client's consciousness is a great healing art.

- *You find the appropriate techniques to use.*

  Some techniques will suit you more than others. You will naturally gravitate to techniques that work for you. There are many techniques to choose from, and you can trust that you'll find the ones that are right for you.

- *The length of a session depends on you.*

  This is an individual matter. Some people work rapidly; others, more slowly. You may like to talk at greater length with clients at the beginning or at the end. This is a matter of individual style. An hour and a half is a good length for these sessions. Do what works best for you.

- *It's important to get permission from your client to do everything that you're doing.*

  If you're going to use healing touch in your session, ask permission. If you're going to work deeply with clients, make certain you ask them if they'd like to do this. It's wise to use a consulting agreement with clients. This will state that you are not diagnosing or treating physical or mental ailments and that you agree to strict confidentiality. If you're a professional, make certain you know the regulations of your profession and your state.

- *Refer clients with serious psychological or medical issues to professionals in these areas.*

    If clients have been hospitalized or are on medication or have chronic issues, refer them to people who have expertise in working with these issues, if you feel this is not within your own realm of expertise.

- *Inform your client about the nature of the work and what to expect.*

    Tell your client about the four phases of the session. Tell her that you'll be doing some deep relaxation and that some people go very deeply; some go very lightly—but that most people are in the middle— that she'll still have full awareness and full control and get the results she needs. Explain the energy therapy work to her—that it's a way of working with the meridian system or energy points of the body and aligning the energy flow. There is more about these explanations in other sections of this book.

- *It's essential that you observe boundaries.*

  It's good to keep references about yourself at a minimum and to keep a professional demeanor. It's also of the highest importance to make certain that, if you're a professional, you refrain from intimate personal relationships with a client.

- *It's good to use your voice in a soothing way.*

  Your voice carries sound vibration, and it's good to be sensitive to how you're sending out that vibration. You might want to ask people you know for feedback on how you're using your voice.

- *Use only those techniques with which you feel comfortable and proficient.*

  You may want to do only energy therapy or only inner healing. You may just want to make tapes for people. You may want only to do this work on yourself. You know what your own being wants for you. It's good to be sensitive to that. Just do what's right for you.

- *Your client can use finger signals whenever necessary.*

  If she is unable to speak because she may be in a very deep state of relaxation (or for any other reason), you may want to offer her the option of using finger signals. You can say, " Which finger would represent your 'yes' finger?" Then watch for her response. "And now which finger would represent your 'no' finger?" Then you proceed to ask questions that can be answered with "yes" or "no"— paying careful attention to the answers, as she raises one finger or the other.

- *Taking notes is a good idea during sessions.*

  It's very helpful to have notes on what your client is telling you as well as on what you're doing to assist her during your session.

- *Discipline your own life.*

  If you're paying attention to your own personal and spiritual growth, you'll find it much easier to be able to hold the space for others. If you do your own inner work, you'll find that you feel more comfortable assisting others when emotions come forth. You'll find yourself more centered and balanced. You won't take on others' issues, and you'll be able to assist them to experience the higher transformational states.

- *Love the people who come to you for assistance.*

  To have an open heart, a sense of high regard for those who come to you, to give them care and love—these are the marks of a loving healer. Yes, it's of great value—and it's professional—to love those who come to you for inner work, as long as that love is from a high place within you. Unconditional healing love is a legacy given to us by the great teachers and masters. It is a quality that is innately ours, as we are reflections of the Divine.

Part Seven

Techniques for Energy Therapy

⟨∽⟩

When you know the tapping "code,"
the doors can open wide.

The technique of energy therapy is so easy, it boggles the imagination as to how it could possibly work. It's about tapping on the right places so that you can open the doors of awareness. If you want to come through any kind of door, you often have to knock. So it is with healing. When you know the "code," the appropriate tapping points on the meridians, the doors can open wide. Here are the steps in the process:

- First you identify the issue you're working on.
- Then you find out how intense it is.
- Next you begin to tap.

There is a special procedure for working with various aspects of the original issue as they arise. You can use these techniques with yourself or with clients. If you're working with clients, you can either tap on them with your own fingers (after obtaining permission), or your clients can tap for themselves.

Identifying and Stating the Issue

It is often best to be clear about what you're tapping for, although some practitioners say you can just call it "this problem" and still get results. Let's get specific for our purposes here. Let's say that you have a headache.

You can call it "this headache." Or perhaps you're dealing with some anxiety ("this anxiety")—or even this very specific "fear that I might not do well on the test tomorrow." (We could call that "this test fear.")

Sometimes you may not really know what the issue is. You feel low in energy, and you may not be able to trace it to that old self esteem issue that is returning; yet as you inquire within yourself, asking yourself or another what it is you're really feeling, you find it. Then you're ready to assess its intensity.

Getting the Intensity Rating

This has often been called the SUDS rating, acronym for Subjective Units of Distress. On a scale of one to ten, with ten being the most intense, how would you rate the intensity level of your issue? This is, as the name suggests, subjective; it comes from within.

Now what if you're not experiencing any issue at the moment? What if you want to work on a fear, for example, that is not happening at the moment, but that comes up when it is triggered by a specific stimulus (a large bridge to cross in your car, for example)? You can close your eyes and imagine yourself experiencing the issue. See or feel that bridge. Feel the emotions that arise as your breathing becomes shallow and your head becomes light. (We've been discussing how inner healing can help you to re-experience these issues so that you can effectively release them.)

Energy Therapy
Emotional Freedom Techniques (EFT)

1. The Setup: While tapping on the side of your hand, the "karate chop point" (see diagram), say: *"Even though I have this (state the problem), I deeply, completely accept myself."* Repeat this "reminder phrase" affirmation three times.

2. The Sequence: Tap five to seven times on the following energy points while repeating the "reminder phrase." As you tap, say. *"This (state the problem.)"*

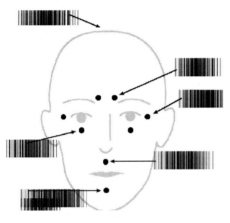

Energy Points

1. Beginning of eyebrow
2. Side of eye
3. Under eye
4. Under nose
5. Under mouth
6. Collarbone
7. Under arm by ribs
8. Top of head
9. Side of hand
10. Inside of wrist
11. Top of hand between last two fingers

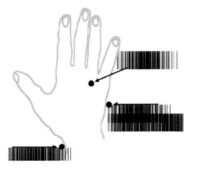

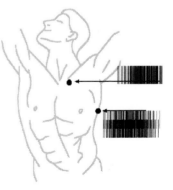

So you get your SUDS rating, and you're ready to begin.

The Setup

The first place you tap is on the side of either hand with what is called the "karate chop" point. This point is found on the outside of your hand, below your little finger, just halfway down the palm. You tap with two or three fingertips of your other hand, medium hard, five to seven times, while saying the following, "Even though I have this (state the issue you're working on), I deeply, completely accept myself." You say this three times, while continuing to tap.

This is called "the setup," and its purpose is to help you handle any internal objections to overcoming your present situation. This reluctance to heal is sometimes called "internal sabotage" or "psychological reversal."

The setup is intended to help you overcome these situations, to override them on an energetic level, so that nothing stands in your way.

The statement says, "…I deeply, completely accept myself," because its purpose is to validate your self worth, so that you can get on with the business of healing.

This first setup in the sequence is done three times.

🌼 The Tapping

One way of doing the tapping is to once again tap medium hard on specific energy points while stating the issue as follows: "this headache" or "my headache." "This fear" or "my fear." "This self-worth issue," etc.

So you say the chosen words (No need to repeat the words, "Even though I have this...", as that is only used for the setup.) Then you begin tapping, saying the key word each time. You tap five to seven times on the following points:

- Beginning of eyebrow at point closest to nose ("This...")

- Side of eye ("This...")

- Under eye on bone (etc.)

- Under nose

- Under mouth on indentation below lower lip

- Collarbone

- Under arm (by the ribs)

- Top of head, just slightly back a bit

- Side of hand again ("karate chop" point)

- Inside of wrist

- Top of hand between last two fingers

Assessing the Intensity Again

At this point, you look carefully at the SUDS rating. It may be down a few points; it may be down to zero—or it may be cut in half. If it's not down to zero, you're ready for another round. You look to see if you're still working on the same issue or if it has changed. Now you begin tapping again, doing the setup only once this time and all subsequent times (not three times as you did in the first round).

Aspects

The issue may be the same, or it may have changed. Your headache, for example, might turn into "this sadness." Your anxiety may turn into "this pain on my left side." Just take note of what is so.

As you do the next round of tapping, you can say, "remaining headache" or "remaining sadness." Go through all the points, and get an intensity rating.

You may find that you get to a zero. If so, you may feel as if your work is complete. If you want to do more (such as affirm positive new possibilities or work with the higher self), see other parts of this book.

⚘ Just Imagine

Let's just say that you have a pain in your shoulder (or your client does). You take a look at exactly where this pain is, and you assign an intensity rating to it. You begin to tap on the side of your hand, saying, "Even though I have this pain in my shoulder, I deeply, completely accept myself." You do this three times. Then you tap on the various points, and you assess the intensity level again. If it's anything above a zero, you begin again, this time tapping on the side of the hand only once, saying, "Even though I still have some of this pain in my shoulder, I deeply, completely accept myself." If the pain has gone somewhere else or if it has changed into something else entirely, you consider the new aspect, which might sound like this: "Even though I have this ache in the back of my head…" or "Even though I feel this confusion…" You adjust accordingly.

Then you tap, and as you do, you say, "remaining pain in my shoulder." Or you say, "ache in the back of my head." Or "this confusion." After tapping, you assess the intensity level until you get to a zero or very low.

You can work with cravings by assessing the intensity of a craving (for any addictive substance, for example) and then by tapping. You can tap on emotions, physical manifestations, repetitive thought processes—on anything at all.

Bilateral Tapping

Feel free also to use either side of the body or both. You can alternate between sides if you like. You can even tap on both sides at once. This process is creative and fulfilling, and you will find that you have been given a gift of a technique that produces results.

It's Easy

This is very simple to do, and you may find that you have instantaneous, miraculous results. With other issues, you may have to keep tapping over extended periods of time. It's good to be persistent, and there are rewards. Remember that you can try it on everything. For some people it works better to have someone else do the tapping. Others like to do it for themselves. You will also find variations on this technique in later parts of this section. You can feel free to combine it with any other modality that you have in your repertoire. Use it freely and find out what possibilities for healing await you.

There are beneficial nuances to know.

As with any discipline, there are some nuances, some fine points, which would be beneficial for you to know. Here, we'll show you some of these. They include ways of dealing with doubt, toxins and internal sabotage, as well as ways of working with intention, forgiveness, reframing and more.

❧ Handling Doubt

If you are a practitioner, you may remember a time when you've completed a session, and you've had successful results. And then your client attributes it to the aspirin she took a few hours before that she says is now just kicking in. This is a response that happens from time to time. It's hard for some people to believe that such a simple procedure could be bringing such monumental results. You can either smile and agree, or you can explain to the person that she just did something that produced results that are remarkable, but true.

❧ Energy Toxins

These are poisons in the system that may be blocking results of the procedures. The toxins can be from something you've eaten, from environmental chemicals, from drugs or alcohol. Ideally the tapping process can help to release you or your client from the effects of these toxins, but sometimes, the toxins serve as impediments, and they put up a barrier in the healing process. If you tap and tap and find you are receiving no results, look for this possibility.

Psychological Reversal

On both an energetic level and on a psychological level, some people have difficulty letting healing come into their lives. We may have secondary gains or subconscious reasons for keeping our problems. This phenomenon is also called internal sabotage, and more often than not, we aren't conscious that it exists in us. We think we wish to be healed; yet there are actual blocks.

There are many reasons people hold onto their challenges. One is that they identify with their problems or pain, and they don't feel safe in letting them go. The problems may have been their ways of controlling their environment. Cigarettes, for example, can provide a literal smokescreen protecting people from thinking old painful thoughts or remembering traumas. They might be ways of grounding or of providing boundaries. And even though people say they want to stop or change, there is something even more compelling inside that locks the problem in.

Whatever their purpose might be, reversals are often illusive and unconscious. One way of discovering what a specific block might be is to ask yourself or your client to complete the following sentence: "I don't want to _____because...." In the blank space goes the supposed desired result. When you answer this without stopping to think about it, you will more than likely hit the jackpot with an answer right away. "I don't want to lose weight because.... I'm afraid of being too attractive (and then I might get hurt or I might change my relationship with my wife/husband or I might not be safe any longer). See more about this in the ReSourcing section (p. 147).

Some practitioners discover psychological reversal with muscle testing. We'll look at that in a moment.

Overcoming such reversal is the primary purpose of the initial tapping on the side of the hand, along with the words, "Even though I have this, _____, I deeply, completely accept myself."

An additional technique for overcoming reversal is to tap on the issue itself. For example, "Even though I want to keep my anger, I deeply, completely accept myself." When you then tap on "want to keep my anger," you can then create the opposite effect, and often the anger will cease to be an obstruction.

Muscle Testing

Many practitioners use muscle testing (kinesiology) to both check for reversal and to see whether a given situation is cleared. There are numerous ways of doing muscle testing. The most common is pressing down on a rigid extended arm of a client. Another is to press on your own rigid forefinger with your middle finger. Still others use techniques they've devised, such as pendulums.

You use strong and weak muscle responses on the body to determine responses to stimulus situations before and after healing.

Here is one way to do it:

Explain to your client that you're getting in touch with her subconscious mind through the strength of her arm muscle. Ask her to sit comfortably and to extend her stronger arm ninety degrees to her body and parallel to the ground. Let her know that you're going to press on her wrist and test her arm's strength. Ask her to simply resist when you press down.

Tell her that you're going to set up this process by an initial "test." You then ask her to repeat after you:

"My name is _____." (You give a name other than her own.) You press on her arm, ask her to resist, and watch it become weak. Do it once again with another name, and press down again. Next use her true first name, and press down. Her arm will most often be strong. Make sure that you remain passive and as detached from the outcome as possible.

After you've set this up, you can now test anything you like. Here are some possibilities for testing weak and strong muscle responses in the energy field. You press down with several fingers on the wrist of her extended arm when you say each of these statements, and you observe whether or not her arm is weak or strong:

"I love myself."

"I'm worried about my future."

"I know I can heal myself."

"I want to stop overeating."

It's an important skill to learn to isolate appropriate issues that might be at the core of your client's process, to find significant statements to test. After you've done your healing process, you can now test to see if her arm and her energy field now test strong.

You can find out other particulars, such as:

"On a ten point scale the intensity of this struggle or emotion is _____."

It's important to remember that muscle testing is not a scientific instrument, but a useful way to establish possibilities to be confirmed by the client's internal experiences.

I have done healing work with little or no muscle testing. Still, there are a number of healers who use muscle testing successfully, and it warrants mention here. If you're interested, there are many books on the subject of muscle testing.

Installing the "Positive"

After you've completed your process, you may want to state the positive while massaging in a circular motion on the energy points. The appropriate words will arise spontaneously from the work you've been doing. Words like "peaceful" or "harmonious" may come forth. You can state the words while massaging the points gently.

The negative polarity is used at the beginning, as it is

an exercise in paying attention to the difficulties. It is necessary to do this in order to place awareness on your experiences. After you've found some resolution, then you can emphasize the positive.

Surrogate and Remote Tapping

There are times when it may be necessary to tap on yourself for the benefit of another. This is particularly true when it involves small children, animals, or those at a distance. There are several ways to do this. While holding the intention to benefit the other, you might tap on yourself, using the first person, "I." For example, one mother assisted her son who was extremely upset. She held him in her arms with his head on her shoulder and said, "Even though I'm feeling upset, I deeply completely accept myself (or, for children, "I really, really like myself"). Then she tapped her own meridians while she tuned into his feeling. The boy's tension and stress significantly reduced.

I've been experimenting in airports and other public places tapping myself for "baby crying" when I hear babies or small children in distress. Without the statistical benefits of a double-blind study, I'd say I have an 80-90% success rate. Most of the children become miraculously quiet.

You can, of course, tap directly on a child or an animal. But in those times when this is difficult, especially when someone is far away, surrogate or remote tapping can be highly beneficial. It's also generally a good idea to "ask permission" of the higher self of the one you're treating.

Intention and Mind Power

Many people have asked whether their own intention or that of the practitioner plays a role in this process. And the answer is most definitely: "Yes." Intention in the world of healing means that the mind or consciousness is clearly focused upon the work being done. This flow of consciousness gives direction to the healing power. When mind and the healing power are in alignment and are focused upon something, the healing power goes to work in a natural even stream of healing that flows from the unseen Source. The one who is focusing the conscious power is then a vehicle for the universal energy to flow through.

In this work with energy therapy, the power of the healing mind is of great importance. It is not simply that the acupressure meridians are tapped or that you are saying the appropriate words. It is that you are connected with the source of healing, and this becomes an intentional process.

Experiments have been done to show the contribution of the energized healing mind. One of the most noted is with the pendulum. The mind can tell it to move a certain way to indicate either "yes" or "no." Amazingly, the pendulum feels the urgings of this charged consciousness and sways to the left, to the right, up and down or in a circle. This is known as "ideomotor action."

In the field of healing, there is always the use of mind power. The everyday mind and ego get out of the way, and the power is turned on enough so that it communicates vibrationally to the recipient. The recipient can be your own self or another. In the tapping, the vibration of the words and the energy in the fingertips or simply in the mental attention can move matter and form in the direction of healing.

This is an important part of the process. It involves bringing one's self into a high state of faith, focusing the mind intently, and getting the ego out of the way to set free a flowing steam of healing energy.

Healing and Prayer

This leads us naturally to the important topic of prayer. It too requires that the conscious mind or ego be moved aside for the moment, and another level of thought that is infused with spirit remains.

In a way, the tapping process, itself, can be seen as a form of prayer. While tapping, you are, in a sense, knocking at the doors of consciousness, "asking" that life situations be released and relieved. These prayers often bring rapid results. The process can be seen as a form of supplication to the universe. It is a way of bringing focused consciousness to bear upon the difficulties of life.

The verbalizations can be seen as requests for results, entreaties to the Self to bring release.

To manifest prayer, we become aligned or harmonized with the universal flow from which the fruits of all requests are received. To do this, we have to get the ego self out of the way, and for this we can use the "setup"— "I deeply, completely accept myself." This is the way of asserting our worthiness of receiving, of removing any egoic impediments to the manifestation of the divine power. We need to balance and open the energy pathways, eliminating any constrictions in our self-worth that could keep the flow from coming. Priests, and others in prayer, by the way, often tap on themselves as they pray: third eye, two collarbone points and heart center.

Origins of the Energy Therapies

A Stanford engineer named Gary Craig developed EFT, Emotional Freedom Techniques. He had a lifelong interest in helping people overcome their emotional limitations. For years, he worked with NLP, Neurolinguistic Programming. Then he discovered the Callahan Techniques, which were later named Thought Field Therapy, the product of many years of intensive research by psychologist Roger Callahan, Ph.D.

In the late 1980s, Dr. Callahan had combined elements of quantum theory, kinesiology and acupressure and had discovered how to apply them to the treatment of emotional disturbance in which he could bring rapid relief for trauma, addiction and phobic disorders.

His first treatment was with a woman who had a severe phobia of water. One day, after a year and a half of conventional treatment, out of curiosity, Dr. Callahan decided to tap her on one of her acupressure points. He'd been studying the body's energy system, and he tapped her on the bone under the eye, a point for stomach distress, as she'd been complaining about discomfort in her stomach.

He was astonished to find that she immediately told him her phobia was gone. She had run to a nearby swimming pool and had begun to splash her face with water. She then ran to the deep end of the pool, and Dr. Callahan stayed close by her for safety. She was able to go into the water, and her phobia was completely gone. It never returned.

Dr. Callahan found that he could create these amazing results with many of his patients. He began to develop and refine his notable discoveries. He created a number of different formulas or algorithms to apply to various issues. The algorithms were quite complex.

In the late 1990s, Gary Craig found that certain meridian spots had been identified as "shortcut" tapping spots, and his work with many people confirmed for him that you didn't need so many algorithms. In fact, he found that a simple method of tapping for everything would be just as good and often, for him, better. He found that the method often works in minutes and can be applied to a wide variety of people, such as children and others who may not want to talk about their issues.

According to Gary, EFT covers "a wide variety of problems with one elegant routine." He feels that all the energy meridians are connected and intertwined so that tapping a few of them sends balanced energy down all of them. He says, "Tapping on the energy system while being tuned to an emotional problem is an extraordinary healing technique that is deserving of the Nobel Prize. Its impact on the healing sciences is bound to be enormous." Gary Craig's web site, www.emofree.com, contains his writings and other information about EFT.

Though they differ on how to do the work, both Gary Craig and Roger Callahan have a similar philosophy on the causes of emotional distress. They believe that thoughts are constantly creating patterns of electrical energy that result in emotional experiences through the release of hormones, neurotransmitters and other chemicals in the body. Thoughts change the body's electrical state. When there is a disruption in the body's electrical flow, we feel it. When the electrochemical disruption is removed, the distress stops. The tapping processes neutralize disruptions in the body's electrical system, which then stops the chemical chain reaction and frees you from emotional and physical discomforts. Gary Craig believes that "the cause of all negative emotions is a disruption in the body's electrical system."

Since these discoveries, others have made their contributions to the field of energy therapy. The variations are numerous (including the combination of hypnotherapy with energy therapy). Some of the other variations are included here as well. It remains to be seen how the work will evolve. Suffice it to say that the contribution is an enormous breakthrough in the field of human transformation.

Energy Therapy Variations

Root Cause Tapping Technique

Based on BSFF, "Be Set Free Fast,"
the Work of Larry Nims

Here is one version of a technique based on tapping specific energy points while using special verbalizations. The original technique has been revised.

- Get in touch with the issue, and state it as clearly as possible.

- Begin with setup: On karate chop point at outside of hand, say: "Even though I have this_____, I deeply, completely accept myself." 3X

- Tap at beginning of eyebrow and say, "I am eliminating all of the sadness in the deepest root causes of this_____."

- Tap under the eye: "I am eliminating all of the fear in the deepest root causes of this_____."

- Tap on back of the baby finger, just in back of nail: "I am eliminating all of the anger in the deepest root causes of this_____."

- Tap on the eyebrow point again: "I am eliminating

all of the emotional trauma in the deepest root causes of this_____."

- Tap under mouth: "…eliminating all of the shame…"

- Tap on top of head: "…eliminating all of the guilt…"

- Tap on the heart center (whole hand or fingers): "…eliminating all of the grief…"

- Then tap on the side of the index finger, and ask client to repeat: "I forgive myself for ever taking this on. I was only doing the best I could. I forgive everyone involved. They were only doing the best they could also. (Specific forgiveness can be done here, as well. If you want, you can even forgive the universe.) I love and accept myself. I am eliminating anything that would make me keep this_____or allow it to come back in any way. I don't need this_____any longer, because I am able to replace my_____with_____." (You can now begin to reframe and speak positively about all the changes that are ready to take place, e.g., "You learn from the experience, and now you see it differently. You understand that_____," etc.)

You may want to use muscle testing to ascertain whether or not each of these steps has been completed. You may not want or need to use testing at all. You may want to get an intensity number from one to ten and see how the number decreases as you work.

TAT
The Tapas Acupressure Technique

How TAT was Developed

Tapas Fleming developed TAT in the course of her
acupuncture practice working with allergies. Many
patients had a particular moment of trauma related to
a food, chemical, or other substance that kept the
allergy in place. She had been working with Dr. Devi
Nambudripad's Allergy Elimination technique when
one day, after a nap, the importance of one particular
acupuncture point that she hadn't been using came to
mind. She tried it out on her next patient and got
excellent results. She kept using the point—actually two
points, one located at each eye—with great success. It
was a useful treatment for allergies, emotional traumas
and physical traumas. After a few months, she showed
the technique to a patient who told her that his T'ai Chi
master had showed him the use of those points plus one
more located between and above the eyebrows—again,
focusing on the eye area. After a few months, while
studying with a colleague who helps heal emotional stress
by having patients do special exercises with the eyes, it
occurred to her that perhaps adding acupuncture points
at the occiput region (back of the head where the brain's
vision center is) would enhance her treatments. It did.
She was now able to drop some steps from her previous
protocol with this new addition of points at the back of
the head.

Theory of TAT

Tapas' basic theory is this: a trauma is a stuck moment that keeps causing stress. In that moment of trauma, some part of you felt, "I can't survive this happening to me." So you said "no" to it. Saying "no" in that original moment creates a tension, because it did happen and some part of you is still telling it "No!" This creates a duality and is called a yin-yang imbalance in Traditional Chinese Medicine. This means that you create "I'm over here and I'm keeping that trauma over there, away from me." This is very stressful because the trauma isn't over there; it's really part of you.

TAT is centered in your eyes. Acupressure is performed on acupuncture points that focus energy on the eyes. By holding these points, you are "re-viewing" the trauma now, and whatever parts of you were saying "no," now say "yes." You know that it is not a threat now. You'll likely feel some subtle shift in your energy as the trauma is now accepted. You will have dissolved the duality of self and trauma. The various symptoms you had were based on which part of your body was resisting that trauma. They'll relax and heal now.

How to Do TAT

First, identify the trauma you want to work on now. This should be one particular trauma, not a long-term relationship or situation. From now on, when the words "your trauma" are mentioned here, it will refer to what you're working on now.

Put your attention on (your trauma).

Rate it at 0-10, 10 being the worst.

Do the TAT pose:

> With one hand, touch thumb lightly just above and adjacent to the inner corner of one eye, fourth (ring) finger above and adjacent to inner corner of your other eye, middle finger touching at midline about one half inch higher than the eyebrows. All touch is light, not pressing. With your other hand, place palm down at the back of the head above the neck and immediately below the occipital ridge (bump at the back of your head) roughly centered at midline.

Put your attention on (your trauma) while in this pose. Remain in this pose until you notice something happen. This is different for each person; often it is a deep sigh. Usually there is a subtle shift of energy which can be sensed as relaxation. Put your hands down.

Rate (your trauma).

Put your attention on the "storage space." This refers to wherever you have been storing the trauma. You do not need to know where that is (for example: weak back, sick stomach, tight jaw, etc.). Your intention to focus on "wherever the storage space was for (my trauma)" works to focus your attention.

Do the TAT pose with your attention on the "storage

space." Remain until you feel a change or one minute passes, whichever comes first.

Rate (your trauma). If it is not a "0," identify what pieces remain. This may be, for example, a particular sound, moment, chemical, food, feeling, physical symptom, thought—whatever is still stuck. If there are more than a few things, it may be helpful to write them down just to remember each one.

Put your attention on each remaining stuck piece, and do the TAT pose, doing one piece after another for a minute or so each till the trauma is a "0" for you.

Drink a glass of water. Drink eight glasses or so in the next 24 hours. It will help the toxins from the trauma to leave.[6]

Rapidly Integrated Transformation Technique

Pay attention to an issue in your own or your client's life. Note your level of discomfort: (0=none; 10=intense). You may also focus on a craving (0=no urge; 10=intense urge). Imagine you are a tree and will be clearing from the branches (the conscious mind) to the roots (the subconscious). As you lightly tap each point using two or three fingers, focus on the issue and read aloud what is in quotation marks.

1. *Universal* (Karate Point—outside edge of hand):

   "I release the problem to Higher Power (God/ Spirit) to transform it and my relationship to it, never to take it back or passively receive it back."

2. *Personal* (Gently massage heart point 3 times in a circle, sore spot above left breast.)

   "I love (accept) myself unconditionally even though I have this problem (or challenge)."

3. *Eyebrow* (Tap either eyebrow where the eyebrow starts, near bridge of nose.)

   "I release all the sadness in all the branches to the deepest roots of this problem."

4. *Under eye* (on bone just under eye, centered)

"I release all the fear in all the branches to the deepest roots of this problem."

5. *Under nose and chin* (Using sides of thumb and index finger, tap both spots at once. Side of index finger will be under nose, and side of thumb will be on chin.)

"I release all the shame and embarrassment in all the branches to the deepest roots of this problem."

6. *Collarbone* (Make a fist, and gently thump below collarbone, on breastbone.)

"I release all the hurt in all the branches to the deepest roots of this problem."

7. *Under arm* (by the ribs)

"I release all the guilt in all the branches to the deepest roots of this problem."

8. *Little finger, side of nail* (Tap on the side of finger next to ring finger.)

"I release all the anger in all the branches to the deepest roots of this problem."

9. *Inside wrist*

"I release all the pain in all the branches to the deepest roots of this problem."

10. Eyebrow (same as #3)

"I release all the trauma in all the branches to the deepest roots of this problem."

11. Index Finger (side nearest thumb)

"I release the energy that has been invested in this problem so I can use the energy for my own well being."

12. Heart Point (massage in a circle, same as #2)

"I forgive myself for forgetting I was doing the best I could." (3 times)

"I forgive _____ (list others, including God) for doing the best he/she/they could." (Do each one individually.)

13. Crown (top of head)

"I bring in Higher Power (Spirit/God/ Light) into all the branches to the deepest roots of this problem."

Breathe. Reassess your level of discomfort or level of urge. If above 0, repeat steps 1-13. When at a zero, continue to step 14.

14. *All spots* (from # 3-10)

"I bring in Higher Power (Spirit/God/Light) to replace the ____ (sadness, etc.) in all the branches to the deepest roots of this problem."

Tap daily (at least three times a day) on any issues that have any emotional charge.

Meryl Beck [7]

Heart Tapping Process

While tapping on your own or your client's heart with both hands, say: "Even though I have this (state the problem), I deeply love and accept myself, God deeply loves me, and this problem is being healed. I am now ready to release this problem." Sometimes any or all of these statements cause hesitation. This shows up where the reversals such as self-hate, not deserving to be healed, or doubt about being able to get healed have been.

Then you can say, "Dear and faithful servant, my subconscious, I ask that you now go down to gather all of the roots and causes of the (problem) and bring them up for deep and complete healing." Often the client is already in tears at this point, and you can continue to tap on the heart until this has passed.

Next you check the SUDS, the intensity rating of the "subjective units of distress." Often at this juncture, the SUDS is down to zero, and another aspect is coming up. If not, you can finish any tapping that may need to be done.

You can also do surrogate tapping with a client, which means that you tap on yourself while a client is tapping on herself. You may instead wish to do the tapping for 7the client. Also, in the earlier tapping, if a person is comfortable with their relationship with God, their angels, guides, etc. you can ask them to join their subconscious in resolving the problem.

Bobbi Sandoz [8]

Working with Reversal

In addition to identifying the negative blocking statements and having your clients tap on those, you can also have them tap on the positive affirmation, particularly if it is one which they do not hold strongly. This is because just saying the affirmation will bring up their negative reaction and thus tapping on it can eliminate some of this charge. It can also bring the inner objections to the affirmations or competing thought forms into consciousness.

You can have your clients say the positive affirmations and rate how much it is true for them on a scale of 1 to 10. If less than 10, have them tap while saying the affirmation. Invariably afterwards it is more strongly held—or we are able to identify negative blocking statements to tap on.

Steve Wells [9]

Release! Method to Emotional Freedom

This technique taps on almost all of the major energy meridians. You first interview your client to determine the issue and the degree of its intensity from 1-10 (or from 0-10, if you like). You then begin the process:

Tapping on the karate chop point, say the material in quotation marks out loud:

"Even though I have this (state the issue)—I accept myself fully and completely." (once)

"Even though I have this (issue), I love and accept myself fully and completely." (twice)

Begin tapping around in a circle at the throat, clavicle, thymus area, saying:

"I love and accept myself even though I have this (issue). Even though I have this (issue), I love and accept myself."

Then, as you say the very same thing, tap in a circle in the opposite direction.

Breathe and release. (From here on, breathe and release any time you determine that it's appropriate, not just the times indicated.)

Begin tapping at the sternum, where the ribs come together, tapping up the chest several times toward the chin.

Say, "Release the (issue)" several times until you reach the chin.

Tapping on these points several times—repeating "Release the (issue)"

> chin
> under the nose
> either side of the nose at the gums
> either side of the nose at the eyes
> under the eyes at the bone
> either side of the eyes at the temples
> eyebrows
> top of the head at the crown

Rubbing the occipital ridge at the base of the skull, say:

"I release this (issue) now. I no longer need it. I let it go now."

Breathe and release

Tap on these points several times, repeating

"Release the (issue)."

> collar bones
> tapping out toward the shoulders
> scapula (as if you're giving yourself a hug,
>   crossing arms)
> inside of a wrist
> outside of that wrist
> side of that wrist

Breathe and release

> inside of thighs at the knees
>
> either side of an ankle (This point may be contraindicated during pregnancy.)
>
> where big toe and the next toe join
>
> either side of other ankle
>
> where big toe and the next toe join on other foot
>
> inside of thighs at the knees

Breathe and release—and pause.

Second Phase of "Release!" Method

Tap on eyebrows saying:

> "I'm eliminating all of the sadness from the deepest root causes of this (issue)."

Pause and rub the spot, saying:

> "I release the sadness."

Take a big deep breath and release, allowing your body and mind to shift and rebalance (after each spot is addressed).

Repeat the same process as above on these following points:

> Under eyes—(Fear)
> Small finger (pinky) near the nail—(Anger)
> Eyebrows—(Emotional Traumas)
> Crown of head—(Guilt)
> Chin—(Shame)

Then, tapping on the index finger near the nail:

"I forgive myself. I did the best I could."

"I forgive myself. I'm doing the best I can."

"I forgive myself for ever putting myself through this."

"I forgive myself for ever taking this on."

"I forgive anyone involved; they did the best they could, considering their limitations."

Pause.

"I forgive myself. I'm doing the very best I can!"

Breathe and release. Pause.

With hand flat on the chest, heart center:

"I'm eliminating all of the grief from the deepest root causes of this (issue)."

Rub this spot repeating,

"I release the grief."

Breathe and release.

Then ask the client to tell you what positives s/he wishes to have in this (heart) spot in place of the (issue).

Often, there will be several words in response.

Then have them repeat:

> "I bring in (whatever they have told you)."

> "I deserve to have (above)."

> "I bring this in for myself now."

Then have them visualize bringing in all of the above positives, feeling those positives flowing into the hand that is on the chest, into the system calming and soothing them.

Be certain to have these positives written down to repeat again to the client when s/he is returning from the relaxation session that follows.

This next step is optional, as your client might be quite relaxed, and you might be ready at this time to begin a deep healing session.

As the client completes the process, ask how he or she is feeling, what might have been experienced, and what the intensity of the issue might be now.

You can tape the "Release!" session so that the client can go through the process at another time on his or her own, following along with the tape.

Kay Heatherly [10]

Making Cassette Tapes about Energy Therapy

One method you can use to increase your clients' connection with the tapping techniques and willingness to use them is to create a special cassette tape for them that includes directions on how and where to tap. You can conclude your sessions with tapes that contain an induction (counting of numbers, attention to breathing, instructions for relaxing, music), and then you can say,

> *And when you relax this deeply, you go to a peaceful place inside of you. And from this place, you realize that you've made an important decision. You've made the decision to* (and here you can restate what you've done together). *You're now able to* (statement of whatever changes are being made).

> *You have many tools to help you.* (Here you talk about the protocol you've discussed in your session.) *And one of these is the ability to tap whenever you need to. You can tap on the side of your hand, your eyebrow and the side of your eye....* (Mention the spots. Sometimes you can also give the instructions for what to say when tapping.)

The point here is to offer the possibility of using tapes to reinforce the client's connection with their healing tools. Clients often say that they listen to their tapes often (sometimes for years), and the exposure to the description of the techniques can certainly assist them. The value of posthypnotic suggestion here is also considerable.

The tapes are short—about twelve to fifteen minutes, and they are easy to do once you get in the flow of it. See p. 193 for more information on tape making.

Marilyn Gordon

Notes

1. Rabindranath Tagore, *Poems of Kabir*, MacMillan India, 1973

2. Kathy Zavada, "Union," Precious Music, 1994 (PO Box 531; Mt Shasta CA 96067)

3. Yogi Ramacharaka, *The Science of Psychic Healing*, Yogi Publication society, 1937

4. John Sanford, *Healing and Wholeness*, Paulist Press, 1977

5. The Peace Abbey, 2 North Main St., Sherborn MA 01770, (508) 650-3659; http://nodes.net? Peace, Room, guest.

6. Tapas Fleming, www.tat-intl.com, tapasvini@aol.com (5031 Pacific Coast Hwy #76, Torrance CA 90505)

7. Meryl Beck, Empowerment Training Center, Mbeck333@aol.com (PO Box 86642, Tucson AZ 85754)

8. Bobbi Sandoz, MSW, SandozB@aol.com, (Hawaii)

9. Steve Wells, Psychologist, wells@iinet.au, (P.O. Box 54, Inglewood, Western Australia 6052)

10. Kay Heatherly, MA, Cht, HeatherlyK@aol.com (4247 Union St., SF CA 94123)

Would you like to learn more?

Worldwide Online Hypnotherapy Email Network:

To participate in a network of people interested in
hypnotherapy and energy therapies, send an email to:
mgordon@hypnotherapycenter.com
with your full name and e-mail address.

Our Web Sites

Check our web sites at:
http://www.hypnotherapycenter.com and
http://www.extraordinaryhealing.com

Some Energy Tapping Web Sites:

EFT Web Site:
http://www.emofree.com
You can purchase videos from Gary Craig, founder of EFT.

Some other energy therapy sites:
http://www. att.net/~tom.altaffer/index.htm
http://www.meridiantherapies.org.uk

For information on Marilyn Gordon's talks,
workshops, intensives, certification programs,
books, tapes and manuals, visit:

www.hypnotherapycenter.com

and

www.extraordinaryhealing.com

To schedule Marilyn Gordon for speaking events, contact:

WiseWord Publishing, Inc.

PO Box 10795

Oakland CA 94606

Telephone: (510) 839-4800

Or 1 (800) 398-0034

Fax: (510) 836-0477

Email: mgordon@hypnotherapycenter.com

Also available from WiseWord Publishing and Marilyn Gordon:

Tapes

Extraordinary Healing spoken word audiotape and CD
Various relaxation audiotapes
Individually-produced audiotapes for your needs
Workshop audiotapes

Books and Manuals

Healing is Remembering Who You Are
"Mind-Body Healing and Habit Control" manual

Certification Programs and Workshops

Regularly scheduled workshops and intensives
offering you the opportunity to become a
Certified Hypnotherapist. A first-rate training program
that gives you skills for doing high quality work,
a "school for your soul."
Special workshops and seminars in "Extraordinary Healing."

Epilogue:
Bringing to Light What's Inside

In your mind's eye, you're diving into a vast ocean of
clear turquoise water. You go very deeply, past the sea
anemones and the coral reefs, down so deeply that you
reach the ocean floor, and here you see a chest. You open
it and find logs and journals of all that has gone before,
as well as brilliant jewels that represent all that might
be. You recognize that everything is here in this very
moment, right now. All that is here in this huge ocean
is teeming with life. You recognize that this is the ocean
of consciousness, itself.

The infinite ocean that exists within human
consciousness is a vast pool of information and wisdom.
Exploring it is an art, and it is central to the whole process
of healing. In it is everything you've ever wanted or
needed to know. Here you find the meanings inherent in
the vicissitudes of your life. You uncover the roots of your
problems. You discover what actions you need to take to
heal. You experience the part of you that is the infinite
observer, and you know that that same part of you is also
united with the universe, itself.

You can open the repository of treasures.

To make these discoveries, you often need to ask
meaningful questions to guide yourself to self-knowledge.

How you phrase the questions is most significant. Here are some ways to open these resources that we've looked at in the pages of our book. You ask yourself or your client:

- Just take a look at that and see what your inner mind would like to show you today. Perhaps it's a picture or a feeling or a thought or an impression. Just see what it is that your deep inner mind wants to experience.

- Let's just see what your wise mind would like to tell you about that experience that you had. Just let your wisdom speak right through you.

- Let's go to the root of that situation that you're experiencing today. The root might take you to another time or place or to a thought or feeling or to another situation you've experienced before. Just let it come forth.

- What is it that you need? How can this be healed?

- If you did know any of this, what might it be? If you pretend you know, what would that knowing be like?

You have a vast capacity to be a vehicle for divine guidance.

Through your own innate wisdom, you can stand back and observe from the expanded perspective. One woman's husband left her, and after exploring her anger, grief, self esteem issues, loneliness, helplessness all of her feelings—and then after embracing the child inside who was afraid, she was led to her Wise Mind. It said to her:

You are experiencing a challenging time now, but you have the strength to handle anything that comes. This is a challenge that is given to you for your growth. There is some deeper causation here, and it is being revealed to you step by step. You have every resource to assist you. You have a guide who is here to give you love and great support. Everything in the long run comes to good, and you will receive many advantages from all that you are handling right now. Just remember, you are truly loved.

This is the divine art of consciousness transformation. First it explores and releases the difficulties. Then it takes you to the next step in your process of coming to light. It calls upon the consciousness that is already within you, and it invites you to experience, release and transform whatever is in the way of your enlightened self. Underneath the "play of light and shadows" is pure consciousness, itself. Underneath the anger, fear, grief, self-doubt, success, failure, rightness and wrongness, there is a radiant core. This is what we've come here to uncover. Fortunately, we have all the necessary tools. Healing is the work of a lifetime, both a commitment and an ultimate joy.

About the Author

Marilyn Gordon is a certified hypnotherapist, teacher, speaker, healer, school director, and author with over twenty five years of experience both teaching and healing in such areas as language arts, meditation, yoga, and hypnotherapy.

She is currently the founder and director of the Center for Hypnotherapy Certification, a California state-licensed hypnotherapy school.

A Phi Beta Kappa from the University of Michigan, she has also been recognized in *Who's Who,...in the US,...in California,...in the West,...in Asia and the Pacific Nations, ...in Executives and Professionals, International Who's Who of Entrepreneurs; Dictionary of International Biography,* and *Outstanding People of the Twentieth Century.* She has been given the Hypnosis Achievement Award for 1997 by the National Guild of Hypnotists, as well as the Charles Tebbets Award in 1999. She writes a regular column for the National Guild's "Journal of Hypnotism."

She has given hundreds of workshops, retreats, trainings and seminars over the years and has regularly appeared on radio and television.

Her area of specialization is in deep inner healing of the mind, emotions and spirit. She also works with and teaches the new leading-edge energy therapies. She does her best to bring compassion, inspiration and love to all she does. Her purpose is to work with love to amplify the good and talents in others, to help them heal mind and body and empower their lives.